#61

Anthony A Williams
AW

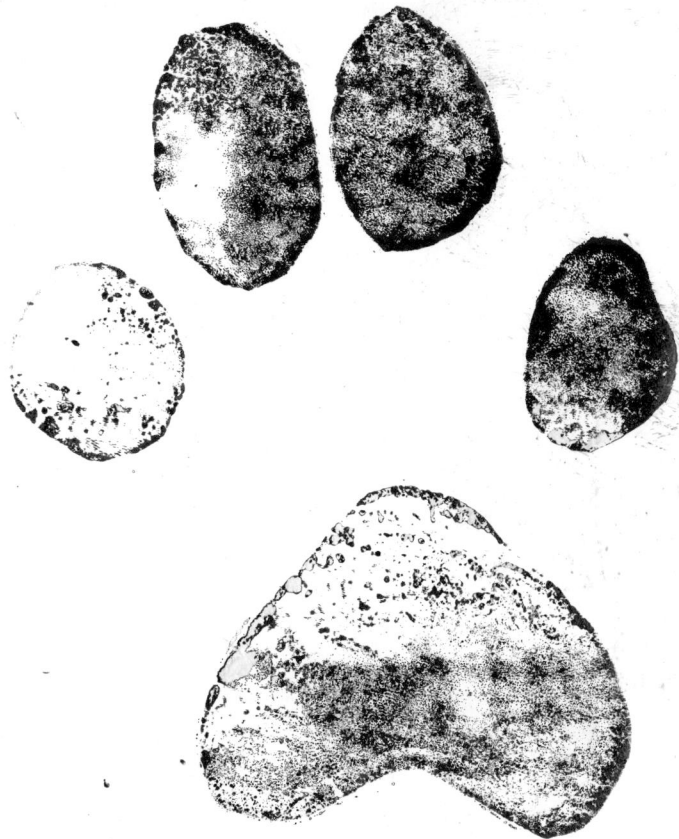

The American Mastiff

Anthony A. Williams

"A gifted photographer whose admiration and respect for the AM breed is transmitted through his camera lens, Anthony's love of Ludo is as contagious as it is obvious. A cherished keepsake and useful resource for anyone who has ever been (or ever will be) touched by an AM, The American Mastiff will find its home on my coffee table for a long time to come." - Desirée C. Kerr, *President and Lead Communications Consultant at Dandelion Consulting Corporation - Toronto Canada*

American Mastiff World Press

Published by American Mastiff World Press, 2110 HWY 337 NW, Corydon, Indiana 47112.
Website: http://www.americanmastiffworld.com/

Author and designer: Anthony A. Williams
Editor in Chief: Desirée C. Kerr
Editors: Carrie Rodgers, Terri Rougeou Donahue, Barb Michalczyk Mecham.
Cover: Ludo, Orion Farms (Merlin X Pandora), born 1 Sept, 2010.
Images by: Anthony A. Williams and Contributing photographers (listed in reference section)

ISBN: 978-0-615-67043-0

Table of Contents

Acknowledgments

I would like to thank all my American Mastiff family members who spent countless hours sharing their pictures, personal experiences and knowledge on this wonderful breed. I would also like to personally thank Missy Nowak for planting the bug in my ear to create this book, as well as my friends and family members who encouraged my every move.

I'd be remiss not to thank the American Mastiff Breeders' Council and the American Mastiff Family Forum for the wide range of information and endless support not only for this book but for the constant well being of the breed. They continually answer questions, address concerns, provide tips and, perhaps most importantly, offer empathy to AM guardians. Having an AM in your life not only adds a large furry kid to your family but also increases your extended family by about a thousand.

My journey writing this book took me all over the country and allowed me to meet a lot of wonderful people. I have to give a special thanks to those who made my journey that much easier: Barb and Larry Mecham; Scott Heaney and Jane Clapp; my brother, Ernest Williams IV; Josh Folmar; Victor Schad and Jessica Zagari; Sara Bell; Rachael Nichols; Mike and Barbara Bradford and everyone else I met along the way who opened their arms to Ludo and me.

Lastly, I have to give a shout-out to my co-pilot, Ludo the Mastiff. He kept me company and even took over driving at times, although turns were a little hard for him with the absence of thumbs, but we survived. He has been my constant rock through a rough patch in my life and his enduring love for me and those around him has never waivered. Yes, I'm aware he cannot actually read this, but he is more than a pet to me. Ludo is my best friend, deserving of every bit of my love and respect and so much more.

Ludo would like to thank all of his friends he met along the way as well. He had an absolute ball meeting new friends, canine and human alike. Playing with other dogs "his own size" was an experience he will not soon forget. Everytime we got back into the car to continue to another state, you could see the excitement on Ludo's face. He just knew it meant he would be meeting a new friend when we stopped. His new friends ranged from a Daschund that stood about seven inches off the ground, to a Wolf-hybrid, tons of American Mastiffs and everything in between. He is constantly asking me if he can do it all again. Maybe one day...

Top: Ludo the AM, Bella the Lab-Pit mix, Lily "Mudpuppy" the Long-haired Dachshund, and Icy the Wolf-Husky
Bottom: Luna the Boxer, the sweetest mooshy-faced girl ever!

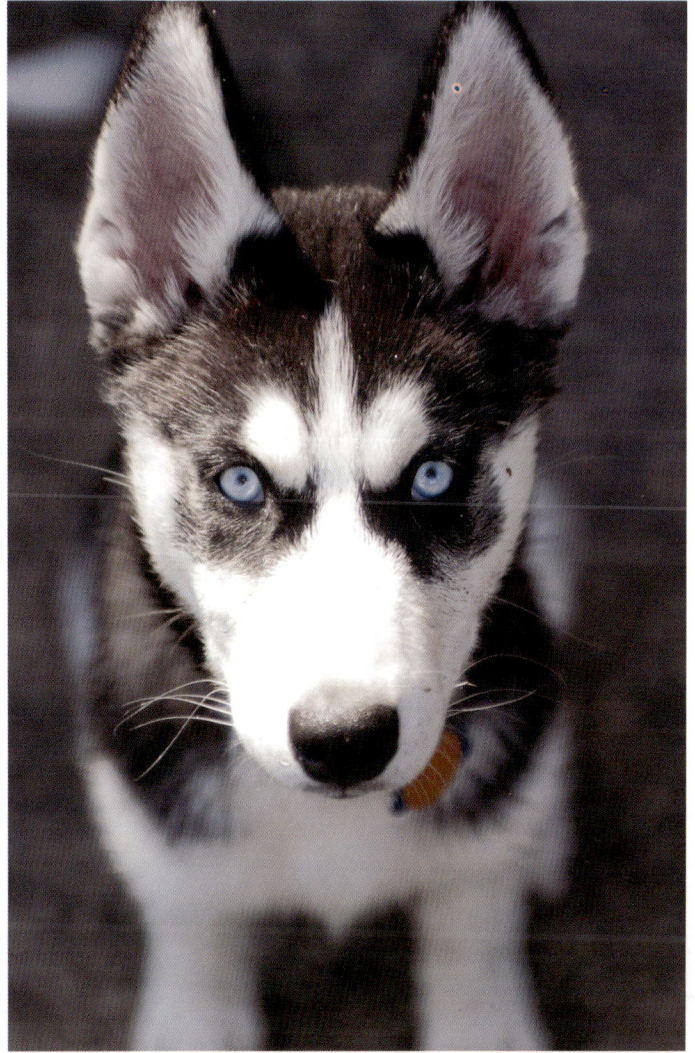

Opposite page: Ludo & Lily "Mudpuppy", the Long-haired Dachshund
Above: (left) Carlos, Ludo's brother (right) Bayo, Ludo's brother-in-law
Below: (left) Rufus, Ludo's uncle (right) Gizmo the cat, Ludo's sister

Breed History and Standard

From Flyingwfarms.com, 2012

The American Mastiff was developed over many years of selective breeding by Fredericka Wagner of Flying W Farms in Piketon, Ohio. The goal was to develop a dog that had the size, temperament, disposition, and the appearance of the Mastiff, but with fewer health problems, and a much dryer mouth than other mastiff breeds. This was accomplished by crossing the English Mastiff with the Anatolian Mastiff during the early development of the breed.

General Appearance: The American Mastiff is a large, muscular, powerful dog with a moderately broad head, dropped ears, kindly wide set eyes, of brown or amber color, the darker the better. Powerful neck, wide, deep chest, muscular back. Tail is wide at the root, tapering to the end, hanging straight in repose, forming slight curve. The overall appearance should be of proportions slightly longer in body than in height.

Size: Height at maturity is typically 32 to 36 inches for males. Males average weight is 160 to over 200 pounds. Height at maturity for females is typically 28 to 34 inches. Females average between 140 and 180 pounds. Larger or smaller for both males and females is acceptable provided the dog is in good proportion and structurally balanced.

Bite: Scissor bite preferred, but a moderately undershot jaw should not be faulted providing the teeth are not visible when the mouth is closed.

Coat: The coat must be short and dense, and of a fawn, apricot or brindle color. However, as in other Mastiff breeds, very rarely a puppy will have a longer coat; this is known as a "fluffy" and is extremely rare but not a fault.

Colors: Fawn, (varying shades from very light cream to darker fawn) also Apricot and Brindle. Brindle should have fawn or apricot as a background color, which should be patterned with dark stripes. Puppies are all born dark and lighten as they grow older, some becoming very light fawn by age one year; some retain dark hairs (not a fault). White on foot, chest, nose and sometimes the chin, is not a fault.

Muzzle: Muzzle should be dark in color, darker the better with same color around the eye orbits and extending upward between them. This is known as the "Black mask". All American Mastiffs must exhibit the black mask in order to meet the breed standard.

Legs: Strong, set wide apart, heavy boned. Feet are large, round, and compact.

Gait: In movement, the gait denotes power and strength; rear legs drive while forelegs track smoothly with good reach.

Temperament: The American Mastiff is a combination of grandeur, good nature, and gentleness. Dignity rather than gaiety. They are neither shy nor vicious. The well-trained American Mastiff is calm, controlled, and confident. Understanding, patient, and loving with their family, especially children. They are generally aloof towards strangers. A well-socialized American Mastiff is friendly yet sensitive and alert to changing situations. They are not aggressive by nature but will defend their family if necessary. They respond to threats with judicious warnings and courageous action if needed.

The American Mastiff looks identical to the English Mastiff in color, shape, size, etc. however, they have a much dryer mouth due to out-crossing early on in the history of the breed. They are very much the "gentle giant." These wonderful dogs love children and are totally devoted to their family. Wise, kind and gentle, they are patient and understanding, very loving with their own people. They are accepting and non-aggressive to your friends, visitors (and the postman), however if anyone threatens their family, especially the children, this dog will gladly give its life defending them.

AMBC breeders insist on puppies going only to loving homes where they will be part of the family. They are easily housetrained using the same training methods used for any puppy. They need to live in the house and be part of the family. They are content and happy when with their family. *Excerpt from Flyingwfarms. com, 2012.*

The American Mastiff is recognized and registered with the Continental Kennel Club (CKC). www.continentalkennelclub.com The CKC recognized the American Mastiff brees as purebreds in January of 2000. Thereafter only offspring of purebred registered American Mastiffs having CKC AR numbers will be accepted for registration as purebred American Mastiffs.

Right: Jazz Bradford

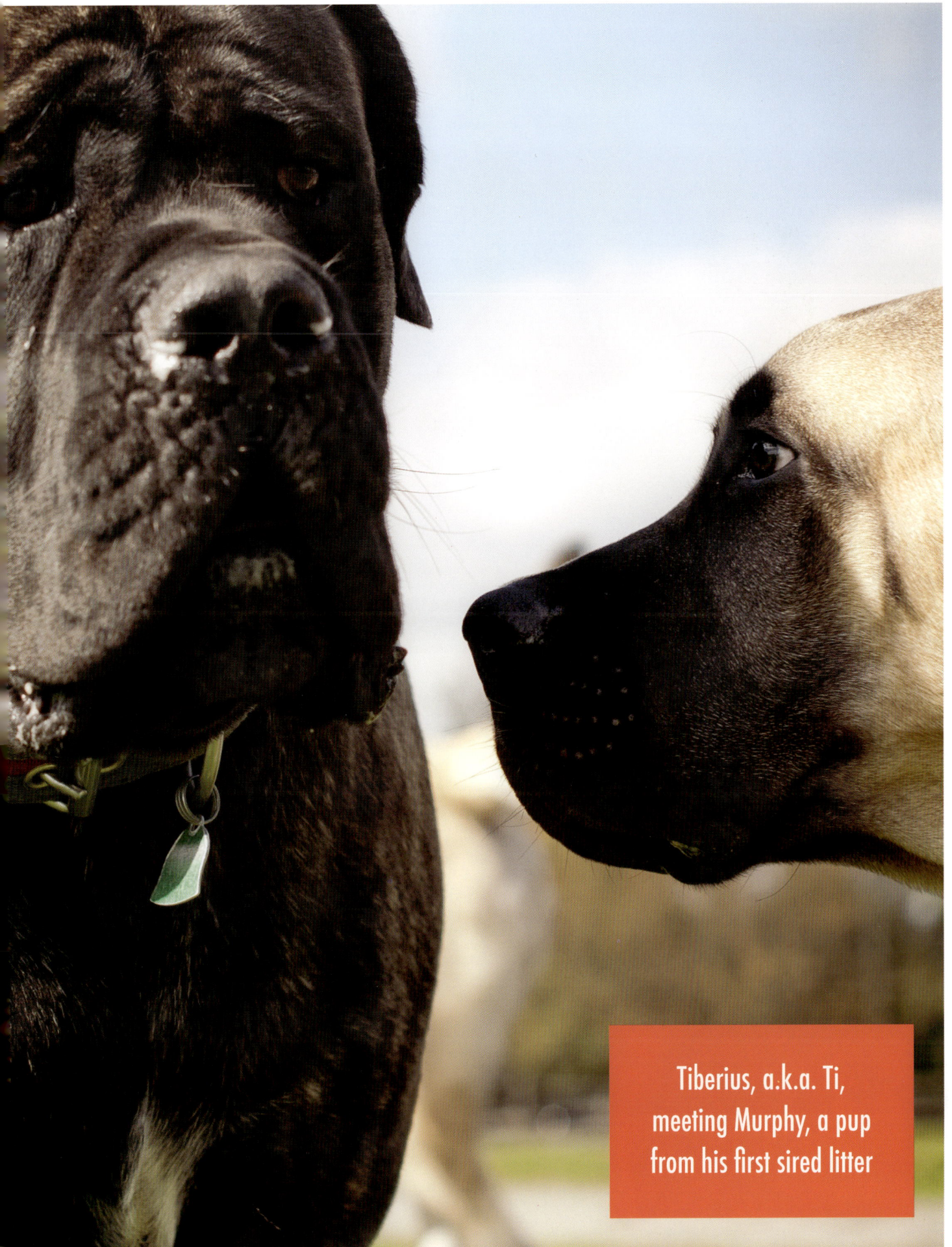

Tiberius, a.k.a. Ti, meeting Murphy, a pup from his first sired litter

Above: Ellie   Below: (left) Aprilia and Optimus Prime, (right) Morgan   Right: Gabby

Maggie May

Maggie is a fluffy AM. Fluffies are a rare throw-back in the gene pool, resulting in a standard AM with longer hair length similar to a Saint Bernard's. Personally, I know only a handful of fluffies and each one of them is unique. These furry kids need a little more grooming than the typical short-coat American Mastiff, but they more than make up for it with their high snuggle factor. While there are pure fluffies and the standard coat length, you will also find AMs in between. Ludo, for example, has slightly longer hair than the norm.

Is an American Mastiff Right for...

You're interested in an American Mastiff. Owning an American Mastiff can be the beginning of a wonderful relationship with years of happiness or it can be the beginning of overwhelming responsibility for which you may not be prepared. American Mastiffs are one of the largest of the dog breeds and can range in size from 29 inches to 36 inches at the shoulder. They weigh anywhere from 130 pounds to 200+ pounds. Once they are over their major growing stage, they will eat between 6-8 cups of high quality food per day.

There are several questions you must ask yourself to determine if you are ready to become an American Mastiff owner. Answer honestly to insure yourself, your family, and your American Mastiff the future you all deserve.

American Mastiffs are wonderful companions. They are not dogs to be left outside chained to a doghouse or to be left alone in a fenced yard. Oftentimes, behavioral problems occur when an American Mastiff is not a member of the family but is relegated to the backyard with

YOU?

only occasional human contact. American Mastiffs desperately need lots of human companionship to be properly socialized, trained, and "owned". If your house is too small for a 130-200+ lb. dog, then an American Mastiff is not the dog for you.

Some American Mastiffs will snore. Are you a light sleeper or one that needs constant quiet to sleep? If so, you may want to consider another breed. Some American Mastiffs will pass gas. Would this offend you? If so, you may want to consider another breed.

For a large breed dog, American Mastiffs are relatively "dry mouthed". Our dogs do not drool except sometimes on the following occasions: when you have an especially yummy treat for them, when they're playing outside on a very hot day, or if they are taking a walk in the woods with a million new smells. And when they get a drink of water, they tend to drink enthusiastically and drip a good bit of water around their water bowl. So if you want absolutely NO drool or mess at any moment in time, you should consider a different breed.

may want to wait until they are older before getting an American Mastiff.

American Mastiffs are NOT guard dogs. They will protect their family more along the lines of a watch dog than guard dog. If your intent is to have a dog that is a guard dog then you must think about another breed. American Mastiffs will bark and let intruders know they are not accepted. Their mere presence and bark will scare the bravest of burglars. Once you accept the guest, chances are good that they will too.

Can I Really Afford To Keep an American Mastiff?

An American Mastiff costs more to maintain than smaller breeds due to its large size and weight. Larger crates cost more. More and larger consumables are needed - food, toys and the like. An adult male American Mastiff can go through 40-70 pounds of dry dog food a month. An American Mastiff, due to its size, will cost you more money at the Vet's office also. The antibiotic for a toy poodle may only cost $10.00 but since most dosages are based on weight, a week's supply of antibiotics for your American Mastiff can cost upwards of $50 to $100. Heartworm medicine costs more, shots can sometimes be more costly, etc.

Do I Have Time To Spend Training, Exercising, And Grooming an American Mastiff?

An American Mastiff should have obedience training. After all, do you want to be pulled down the street, legs streaming behind you, when your 185 lb. male wants to chase that squirrel? The obedience training must be the positive reinforcement type. American Mastiffs are very sensitive to the reactions of their people. Most American Mastiffs can be absolutely crushed by harsh words. They respond well to love, praise, and especially treats. The training should not be negatively based.

But honestly, our dogs live in the house with us and I personally consider them non-droolers.

American Mastiffs are wonderful with children. They are very gentle and quite tolerant of ear and tail pulls, sitting on their backs (not a good idea), and they adore licking kids faces. They will protect their children. However, the swinging of an American Mastiff's tail can knock a small child over. If you have very small children who are just learning to walk, you

Left: Rocco Right: Gus

An American Mastiff should be extensively socialized. This includes taking your puppy (and later dog) as many places as possible to expose it to many situations, many different people, and many different dogs. Proper socialization takes A LOT of time and effort. If you do not have extra time to devote to socializing your new puppy, you should not purchase an American Mastiff.

Exercising an American Mastiff is not as difficult as exercising one of the various sporting breeds who seem to have endless energy. An American Mastiff is happy to go on 2 walks a day of about 20-30 minutes. Some love to hike and swim, but jogging companions they are not! You should not take them jogging as it can be very difficult on their joints. About a mile or so walk twice a day is enough unless it's an older American Mastiff, then play it by ear. Remember, American Mastiffs are like some of us... a couch is their idea of the perfect place to spend a day but exercise is important to keep them fit and help them live longer.

Grooming an American Mastiff is very easy. One to two times per week with a shedding blade or comb is sufficient. It only needs a bath when it begins to smell "doggy" (once a month is more than enough) or if it has gotten into something that needs to be washed off. Bathing an American Mastiff is sort of like washing a hairy Volkswagen except that the VW won't shake and drench you in shampoo or rinse water. Cutting nails is important and should be done regularly. It should be started early in life as wrestling with a large dog is very interesting! Teeth cleaning should also be done regularly.

Will an American Mastiff Fit Into My Lifestyle And My Home?

No matter what, an American Mastiff wants to be with you. They are devoted to their owners and want to have contact with them frequently. They will follow you from room to room as you do your work. Some want to touch you all the time. Do you own a big car or van so your dog can go for rides with you to the park, beach, post office, Vet's office, etc?

As stated earlier, an American Mastiff is a house dog. A small house is suitable as long as the dog goes for walks and plays outside.

The yard should be fenced and the American Mastiff obedience-trained through the basics: come, sit, stay, down, and he should walk on leash without dragging you down the street.

Within your home, American Mastiffs need a place of their own where they will feel comfortable and secure, just like any other dog. Crates are a practical solution, especially for puppy house training and safety. Wire crates are best so that the pup can see out and because they are harder to chew or destroy. Purchase the largest one you can afford so your American Mastiff can grow into it. A dog bed by your bed is also a good idea since they want to be with their families and it is preferable not to let them sleep on the bed with you. Jumping off of a bed is not good for the joints when they are young, and when they get older, space could be an issue!

Are you trying to talk me out of getting an American Mastiff?

Yes and No.

No, because it would be wonderful if everyone could experience the joy and satisfaction of being owned by one of these Gentle Giants.

Yes, because as great and wonderful as they are, American Mastiffs are not the right breed for everyone. It would be much, much better if you found out that a Mastiff wasn't the breed for you NOW instead of after you've already gotten one.

American Mastiffs are giants and take up a lot of space on the couch and in the house and car. They have powerful tails that can clean off a coffee table in one fell swoop or knock a small child down with one wag. They like to be close to their family and will sit on your feet, lean against you, often put their paw on you and lay their heavy head in your lap. They like to follow you wherever you go and be part of whatever you do. They can block doorways with their huge bodies, stand in front of the TV and block your view, and take up large amounts of space with their crates and toys.

If you can't handle any of the above, then an American Mastiff is not the dog for you!

American Mastiffs need to be properly socialized and trained. Do you have time to devote to taking your American Mastiff many different places, introduce it to a variety of people and dogs? Do you have time to attend training classes with your puppy/dog? If you are a very busy person who doesn't have a lot of free time to devote to your dog, then an American Mastiff is not the dog for you!

American Mastiffs are not guard dogs, they are watch dogs. They know the difference between friend and foe and pick up on the emotions of their owners. They possess the natural ability to defend their family should the need arise. American Mastiffs are not recommended as a guard dog for businesses or junkyards because of their instinctual need to bond with people. The American Mastiff temperament is not suited for formal "guard dog" training due to their sensitive nature and because to do so may permanently ruin their temperament.

These are large dogs. They shed an average amount, but they are large and thus have a lot of hair to shed. And they are messy when they drink water. If you like a perfectly clean house at every moment, you should consider another breed.

If you are on a tight budget or do not enjoy spending money on your dog, please reconsider getting this breed. The initial purchase price of the pup will be the least expensive part of owning an American Mastiff.

However, if you've taken all this into consideration and you are ready for a dog who will love and adore you and your family members for all of its life, one who will make you feel like you are the most special person in the world, one who would do anything within its power to make you happy, then an American Mastiff would be a wonderful addition to your family!

If you have not met an American Mastiff in person, we highly recommend visiting a breeder or an owner near you so you can meet this wonderful breed to help you decide if this is the perfect breed for you and your family.

Owning an American Mastiff is a major responsibility, but they will reward you a million times over with their love. *Excerpt from Deepwood Acres [www.deepwoodmastiffs. com], 2012.*

* Note from Anthony: My American Mastiff, Ludo, and my first one, Lurch, are the best dogs I've ever had, but they aren't without a ton of responsibility. It takes hard work, time, patience, and money to enjoy the comforts of their big sloppy kisses.

Left: (top) Optimus Prime (bottom) Vayda Below: Murphy

Gus and Ludo demonstrate a typical play-bow which means "let's play!

Owning an AM

The true cost of owning an AM.
When a person meets an American Mastiff out on the town, they assume they cost a fortune to buy and feed. Since I'm often asked, "how much did you pay for him", I have prepared myself for the answer along with additional information to be supplied with my response. After I tell them how much Ludo's adoption price was, I then let them know that the $1600 is the lowest adoption fee offered by the AMBC breeders but this initial payment represents one of the smallest costs you'll encounter throughout the life of your AM. While this list and the associated costs varies greatly from family to family, it's a good start when considering what to expect and budget.

- Adoption fee: $1600 - $2000
- Trip to get your new AM: $0-$1000
- Puppy essentials (bowls, collars &leash, toys, crate, bed): $300 - $400
- Typical veterinary bills (shots, neuter/spay): $200-$600
- Non-typical veterinary Bills (injury, illness): $100 - $6000
- Food + treats: $75 - $200 per month
- Health Insurance: $50 - $100 per month
- Parasite preventatives: $40 - $70 per month

First year estimations: $3235.00 based on averages, without any accidental or illness related vet bills or health insurance. This could be lower for some, higher for others.

These prices are not to scare you, but to help you realize that having a 150 to 250 pound furry kid running around your house is a lot different then a five-pound lap dog in terms of prices. Families who are considering adding the absolute joy of an American Mastiff to their pack MUST be ready to do what's best for their boy or girl, and it isn't cheap.

This also does not mean there aren't ways to have an AM as part of your family with a more practical budget, but the idea here is to demonstrate the possible financial issues that come along with giant breeds. The bigger they are, the more they cost.

Left:

Ludo slinging some drool while playing with his friends, Gus and Brutus, just outside of Pittsburgh

A public figure: Having an American Mastiff comes with a lot of work as well as a lot of perks. Once you have invited one of these love bears into your home and heart, you will never be without attention again. Socializing your new pup, as discussed earlier, is super easy since everyone on this planet will want to come up and say hi to your dog. For this reason, I feel it is only fair to prepare you for the things you will be asked OR told while out on the town with your big boy or girl. Here is a list for your entertainment and preparation:

- Is that Marmaduke, or, is that a Great Dane?

- Can you ride that thing?

- You could put a saddle on that.

- Is that a Bull Mastiff?

- What is he/she mixed with?

- I bet they eat a lot.

- What do you feed him/her?

- Is he/she friendly?

- How much did you pay for them?

- Do they slobber a lot?

- Do you walk them or do they walk you?

- How big is your car?

- That's a HORSE!

- That's the biggest dog I've ever seen!

- What's their name?

- I'm scared!

- Can we pet them?

- Can I take a picture with them?

- You must have a big house/yard.

And be prepared for all around pandemonium when you are out in public events with your AM. You could be at an autograph signing for Brad Pitt and guess who will steal all the attention? That's right...your furkid! I would put money on my Ludo getting WAY more love than Brad Pitt if they were in the same place. Hell, he would get love FROM Brad Pitt.

The bottom line is, owning an AM is like becoming a personal assistant to a celebrity. You won't be able to go anywhere there's a crowd of people without being stopped every five feet for questions and pictures. If you really want to look at the art during an art festival, then plan on being there for a minimum of five hours if you bring your pooch along. I'm not going to lie, I personally love the attention my boy Ludo gets. The only downside is, he now has a complex where he thinks everything and everyone is on this earth to pet him. To a certain extent, he is right!

Right: Sasha and Jed , the Golden, staying safe during hunting season
Below: Duval, Ludo's full sister wih her brother Cooper

Above: Winnifred vs. Godzilla
Right: Titan, an AM in the Philippines
Far Right: Ludo and Vic (6'5, 225 lbs)
Below: Samson.

Frequently asked questions:

What breeds were used to create the American Mastiff?

Approximately 20-25 years ago, Fredericka Wagner of Flying W Farms in Ohio, crossed an English Mastiff with an Anatolian Mastiff. Through years of very selective breeding, the American Mastiff was developed.

Why was the American Mastiff created?

Fredericka Wagner was a very respected English Mastiff breeder for many years. She sought to minimize some undesirable traits in the English Mastiff, mainly excessive drooling and health problems, including a high incidence of hip and knee problems and short lifespan, among others. The result is the present-day American Mastiff. The American Mastiff is similar to the English Mastiff in size, appearance, and temperament. Because of the early outcross and very selective breeding, on average, American Mastiffs tend to drool less than their English Mastiff cousins, have a lower incidence of health problems (although they are not completely immune to giant breed health issues), and tend to have a longer lifespan.

What is the AMBC?

"AMBC" is an acronym for American Mastiff Breeders Council. The AMBC consists of 10 approved American Mastiff breeders in the United States, Canada, China and the Philippines. These breeders have voluntarily agreed to abide by the ethical breeder guidelines and rules of the AMBC. These are breeders of the true purebred American Mastiff dogs which trace their bloodlines back to Flying W Farms, Inc. (www.FlyingWFarms. com), Fredericka Wagner, Breed Founder.

www.americanmastiffbreederscouncil.com

What do American Mastiffs look like?

The American mastiff is a large, muscular,

29

powerful dog with a moderately broad head, dropped ears, kindly wide-set eyes of brown or amber color (the darker the better). The neck is powerful. The chest is deep and wide. The back is muscular. The tail is wide at the root and tapers down to the end and hangs straight in repose, forming slight curve. The overall appearance should be of proportions slightly longer in body than in height. All American Mastiffs must exibit the black mask to meet the breed standard.

Are there different colors of American Mastiffs?

Fawn, (varying shades from very light cream to darker fawn), also Apricot and Brindle. Brindle should have fawn or apricot as a background color which should be patterned with dark stripes. Puppies are all born dark and lighten as they grow older, some becoming very light fawn by age one year and some retain dark hairs (not a fault). To meet the breed standard, all American Mastiffs must have a black mask, the darker the better. White on a foot, chest , nose and sometimes the chin is not considered a fault.

While Ludo walks nicely on a leash, Carlos has a sled dog mentality. To make it easier, Ludo gets to walk Carlos. Ludo is only in front of Jamie, Carlos' mother, for visual effect.

Above: Vayda with her mom, Missy

The average female weighs between 140 and 180 pounds. Larger or smaller for both males and females is acceptable, provided the dog is in good proportion and structurally balanced.

What is the temperament of the American Mastiff?

A "Gentle Giant," the American mastiff is a combination of grandeur, good nature and gentleness. Dignity rather than gaiety. They are quite, calm, loving, and loyal. They are neither shy nor vicious. The well-trained American Mastiff is calm, controlled, and confident. They are understanding, patient and loving with their family, especially children. They are generally aloof towards strangers. A well-socialized American Mastiff is friendly yet sensitive and alert to changing situations. They are not aggressive by nature but will defend their family if necessary. They respond to threats with judicious warnings and courageous action if needed.

Do American Mastiffs get along with other pets in the household?

As with any other breed, if the American Mastiff is socialized early with other pets in the household, there is no reason they cannot coexist peacefully and even become great friends.

Are American Mastiffs indoor or outdoor dogs?

American Mastiffs are indoor dogs. They need to be with their people to be happy and mentally healthy. They, of course, love to run around the yard and go for nice walks, but they must live in the home with their family.

Do I need to have a large home?

American Mastiffs do just fine in an apartment with daily exercise. A daily walk or two will do. If you have a fenced yard, your AM will be happy to run around. As they grow older, American Mastiffs may tend to become a little lazy. They are relatively inactive indoors ("couch potatoes").

How big do American Mastiffs get?

Height at maturity is typically 32 to 36 inches at shoulders for males. The average male weighs between 160 to over 200 pounds. Height at maturity for females is typically 28 to 34 inches.

31

Do American Mastiffs require a lot of exercise?

American Mastiff puppies are as active as any other puppies, but are inclined to be lazy as adults. They will keep more fit and be happier if they are given regular exercise. Like all dogs, American Mastiffs should be taken on regular daily walks to help release mental and physical energy. It's in a dog's nature to walk. As with any dog breed, they should always be leashed for their protection while in public.

Do American Mastiffs shed?

American Mastiffs are average shedders. They tend to shed twice per year. Periodic bathing and brushing will minimize any accumulation of fur in the household.

Do American Mastiffs drool?

On average, American Mastiffs tend to drool less than their English Mastiff cousins. The "drool factor" does vary between individual dogs, with reports of some dogs drooling minimally and other dogs not drooling at all. Some AMs drool only after running on a warm day or in anticipation of a yummy treat.

Do American Mastiffs snore?

Many, not all, American Mastiffs snore. Please keep this in mind when deciding whether an American Mastiff is the right breed for you, as AMs want to sleep in the same room with members of their family.

Are American Mastiffs gassy?

Mastiffs are known to be gassy. Just as in humans, some diets are better tolerated by some and not others. Experimenting with different high-quality foods may result in less gassiness.

Are American Mastiffs difficult to train?

American Mastiffs are very intelligent dogs. There is never a need to raise your voice with your American Mastiff. They are very sensitive

and respond very well to a normal but firm and confident tone. Positive reinforcement is the best method of training for the American Mastiff. They can be stubborn at times and require consistency in training. If you are a first-time large/extra-large dog owner, formal training classes are firmly recommend with your pup to help train you along with your American Mastiff. Not only will you learn plenty of great techniques and have the opportunity for your American Mastiff puppy to socialize with other dogs and other people in different surroundings, you will have an awesome bonding experience with your pup! Puppies of all breeds go through some difficult phases while growing up, and consistency in training is of the utmost importance. I feel that proper socialization and training is even more important for large and extra-large breeds. It might be "cute" for a 20-pound dog to greet you at the door by jumping up on you, but it certainly isn't "cute" for a 200+ pound dog to do the same. It is never enjoyable to be around an un-trained or under-trained dog, but it is always a joy to be around a well-trained and well-mannered dog!

Note: There are lots of different training methods (and trainers) available. Please investigate thoroughly and check references, and choose the trainer and/or facility that best suits the needs of you and your pup. Don't be afraid to ask questions!

If you choose to train your American Mastiff on your own, keep your training sessions short (about 15 minutes or so at a time). Never raise your voice to your American Mastiff. A normal but firm tone is much more effective. Reward your puppy with lots and lots of praise (and treats if you do so choose). Make the training sessions fun, but not overwhelming. Focus on only one or two commands per session until each is mastered. Practice daily. Remember, consistency is key.

How quickly do American Mastiff puppies grow?

American Mastiff puppies grow very quickly.

You will notice that they eat and then sleep A LOT. On average, puppies gain between three to five pounds per week for their first eight months or so. Because they can't possibly eat enough at one sitting to sustain themselves for more than one hour at a time, it is recommended that they be free-fed so they can eat throughout the day.

Because American Mastiff puppies grow so quickly, great care must be taken to ensure that their joints and bones are protected from injury. American Mastiffs puppies must not be over-exercised. This means no jumping off anything higher than 12 inches or so, no major "rough-housing" with people or other pets, and no excessive running or quick turns.

It is a good idea when training your relatively young AM puppy to use a ramp to get in and out of your vehicle. Once they become too large to safely lift, it will become potentially dangerous for both you and your American Mastiff to try to lift him/her into your vehicle.

After the first year, their growth rate begins to slow down. You will notice growth spurts in your American Mastiff by the sudden increase in appetite. American Mastiffs grow "up" (tall) for the first two years and "out" (fill out) for the next two years. American Mastiffs are not fully grown until four years of age.

Is it expensive to own an American Mastiff?

As a general rule, a larger dogs cost more than small dogs. Larger dogs require larger quantities of vaccine, heartworm and flea and tick prevention and other medications (as they are based on weight). Extra-large dogs require more food, larger crates and larger beds, which cost more than smaller-scale items. Boarding/kenneling extra-large dogs costs more also. Don't forget, you'll need a vehicle large enough to transport your extra-large dog comfortably.

Is socializing my American Mastiff important?

Socialization is a very important aspect of

every dog's development. It is very important to expose your American Mastiff to lots of people of both sexes representing different ages and colors, other dogs and other animals, as well as different places and situations in a positive manner. Well-socialized dogs tend to be friendlier and less fearful of the kinds of individuals they were socialized to. Don't underestimate the importance of continued socialization of your dog well into adulthood. Dogs need continued socialization throughout their lives.

Are American Mastiffs good "watchdogs?"

Because of their sheer size, American Mastiffs are a very good deterrent for any potential criminal. American Mastiffs are extremely intuitive when it comes to threats. If an American Mastiff senses a potential threat, he/she will stand between their loved one and the potential threat until they feel that their loved one is safe. They will defend their loved ones with their lives, if necessary.

Can I register my American Mastiff with the American Kennel Club (AKC)?

No. This line is relatively new, so it is ineligible for registration in most breed registries. Registries with less stringent requirements may recognize a new breed with recent history, such as the Continental Kennel Club's recognition of the American Mastiff line in 2000. American Mastiffs were bred to be family dogs, not show dogs.

Can I show my dog at dog shows?

No. American Mastiff breed was solely created to be family dogs, not show dogs. The American Mastiff breed is not registered with the AKC, making them ineligible to be entered in any AKC sanctioned shows.

*This section is from the AM Family Forum (http://amfamilyforum.net). *Note from Anthony: There are non-AKC shows that would be great for showing off your American Mastiff. These can include Rally and Obedience competitions.*

Murphy and one of his brothers.
Notice how Murphy already knows who's in charge.

34

Bringing Home Puppy

To be prepared for your new American Mastiff puppy, you must have certain items ready. You'll need a crate if you are planning on crate training. The size of crate needed will depend on how long you plan to crate them. I had the XXL crate and Ludo filled it up by around six months of age, at which time I started to allow him to roam the house one room at a time. Which brings me to the next necessity, baby gates. You'll want to always keep an eye on your puppy to ensure potty training goes smoothly. Baby are a great tool to help with this and are especially practical when you have house guests or when you are ready to introduce your pup to each room of your house as he or she matures. Eventually you won't need them, as your pup will be fine roaming the house, but until you have complete confidence, baby gates will save your life. Ludo was totally trustworthy around a year old. I trust him anywhere now.

You will also need food and water bowls in place before bringing Puppy home. I like the elevated ones that move from the floor up to 18 inches or so, since these allow you to raise them as your pup grows. There is still debate whether elevated food dishes aid in the prevention of bloat, but I know Ludo sure likes them, especially for his water. He gets his food outside since it is whole, raw prey animals, but even then he tends to pick them up, hold them in his mouth, and chomp on them in a full standing position until he's finished.

Food is imperative since these little boys and girls pretty much just eat and sleep for the first part of their lives. It is said that when they are sleeping, they are dreaming about their next place to sleep. Find out what food your breeder is using and stock up until you decide if you want to switch. If you decide to switch your pup's diet, ensure you have enough of the original food to allow for a slow transition to the new type. This transition should take place over the course of a couple of weeks, gradually increasing the proportion of the new food to help your pup adjust and to avoid tummy upset (occasionally, somewhat affectionately, referred to as "cannon butt").

Free feeding is recommended for growing pups since they need a varying amount of nutrients throughout the day. Free feeding is optimal if you decide to feed kibble. If feeding a raw diet, then feed a minimum of four times a day and stick to the rules of raw feeding for giant breed puppies. Once they are older, a once-a-day feeding schedule is optimal. Plenty of information is online for this type of feeding program.

Soft bedding for your crate is another must, although this could just be thick piles of old blankets, a trampoline bed, or anything else that you would feel comfortable sleeping on.

Remember to bring a leash and collar with you when you pick up your new family member. Some breeders send their puppies home with collars and some don't. Ask your breeder when you make your pick-up appointment so that you are prepared in either case. If you are flying to get your pup be sure to have an

Ludo!
This was the first time Ludo and I met. He was five weeks old at Orion Farms' open house.

Aprilia: Dan and Monica Spilman adopted Aprilia after learning of her rough start in life. As an infant, she was expected to go blind due to eye infections, but with the help of Orion Farms and the Spilmans, she now has 95% vision and is an amazing "little" big girl !

airline approved soft crate, since you'll want to fly with your pup at your feet instead of down below with the luggage. I do not recommend flying in the luggage area at all for puppies in general.

Last but not least, you will need toys! Make sure you select lots of varied toys, including soft, hard, gummy, rope, fabric and other materials to keep teething Puppy's mouth busy. Having a variety of toys will keep your shoes, safe, too! Always supervise your pup's playtime with his or her toys to ensure safety.

The first few days you have your new furkid home will be the most hectic. Getting into a good routine will help minimize stress and shorten the time it takes to potty train. There are leashes out there that wrap around your waist and connect you to your dog. These can be used to help keep an eye on your little one.

The rule of thumb for potty training is to take your pup out when they wake up from a nap, after they eat or drink, and after they play for awhile. A puppy's bladder cannot hold urine like an adult dog. It's not until around six months of age that puppies gain full control of their bladder functions. Until you are confident in their ability, stick with the routine as if they were new puppies. With a consistent routine, AMs are house trained very quickly. I used the bell technique, where I hung bells by the back door and taught Ludo to ring them when he wanted to go out. It took about four days and he was ringing away. You can go to poochie-pets.net to see what I use. They come with instructions that work like a champ!

Begin socializing your pup to people and animals from day one, making your furkid's health your first priority. Do not expose them to areas with an increased risk of contagious diseases (such as dog parks, pet store floors, or anywhere with dog excrement). Being smart about where you take your dog is important but so is socializing him/her. There is a small window of time available to instill the basics about socialization in training so take full advantage of it. American Mastiffs like all

people and animals if socialized correctly. Ludo, in my opinion, is overly socialized, if that is possible. He loves everything and thinks everyone is supposed to pay attention to him and play. This is great with humans, but can be an issue with other dogs. Some dogs are not social, and Ludo does not care in the least bit. He will still walk right up to them to say, "hi, play with me, please" and they may snap at him. I'm working on getting him to ignore dogs in public now, for this reason. It would've served him better if I had approached this aspect of socialization when he was younger, but it is never too late to learn! As with any breed of dog, if left outside or without much contact with humans and other animals, dogs will behave accordingly. This in no way reflects the traits of ANY breed, but merely shows the lack of parent responsibility. So please, socialize, socialize, socialize, smartly.

Training can also begin as soon as you bring your puppy home. I wouldn't work on obedience right away or expect too much out of your little one, but manners and house rules should be taught from day one, slowly but surely. Begin researching trainers in your area and find the one that works best for you and your dog. Although AMs can be a bit stubborn at times (ok, a lot stubborn at times), they are very bright and pick up training very easily. Consistency and praise is the key! These pups love, love , love affection and treats, so go nuts with love, but do not fear appropriate corrections if your trainer recommends it. In the end, it's your dog and you need to do what you feel comfortable with. Ludo has done well with positive reinforcement but has also needed corrections at times. He is the most bull headed AM I've ever met, but also the most well behaved dog most non-AM people have ever met. American Mastiffs tend to have this same nature, but they still need the nurturing from their humans in order to succeed.

Nighttime can be the most frustrating time for new AM owners, or any puppy parent, for that matter. The sleepless nights of whining and crying gets old quickly, but there is good news. Not all AM pups whine at night; some literally do sleep straight through with the occasional potty break. Others are total babies and the fact that they are away from their original pack drives them nuts. Here is a cure that worked like a charm for me. The first week your pup is home, plan to not sleep in your bed. Make something comfortable for yourself next to the crate your puppy will sleep in. The first couple of nights, sleep right next to the crate so your furkid can see and smell you. The whining should be minimal with you being this close. As the days go on, begin to increase the distance between you and the crate. By the end of the week, you should be sleeping by "your" bed instead of theirs. After the week, you should be able to move back to your cozy bed without a peep from your little one, with the exception of potty break whines. They will need to go out in the middle of the night or really early in the morning. Of course, you could choose to totally ignore the whines and they will get over

it, but I'm a light sleeper and the terror that came from my pup's vocal chords was enough to turn me into an Edgar Allan Poe character. Needless to say, I sacrificed my pillowtop for some much needed rest.

With these basics your first week with your new pup should be fun, exciting, and a breeze. I can tell you, out of all the breeds I've had growing up and as an adult, my American Mastiffs have been the easiest puppies I've ever raised or known!

My Honda Fit is the best car I've ever owned when it comes to balancing space and fuel efficiency. It can comfortably hold two adults and two fully-grown AMs

Start shopping for size appropriate vehicles BEFORE you bring home your AM puppy!

Below: Gabby Right: Ruthie

Sisters, Islay and Roka

American Mastiffs grow much more quickly than most dogs. When you bring your new fur-kid home at around eight weeks of age, he or she will weigh 15 - 20 pounds. AMs put on about five pounds per week for the first year. For the first two years, AMs grow tall and skinny (much like a goofy teenager); for the next two years, they fill-out and settle into their healthy adult frames. In this book, you get to see AMs at many stages of growth. The skinnier ones are more than likely still pups. Even Ludo is not yet two years old in his newest images throughout this book.

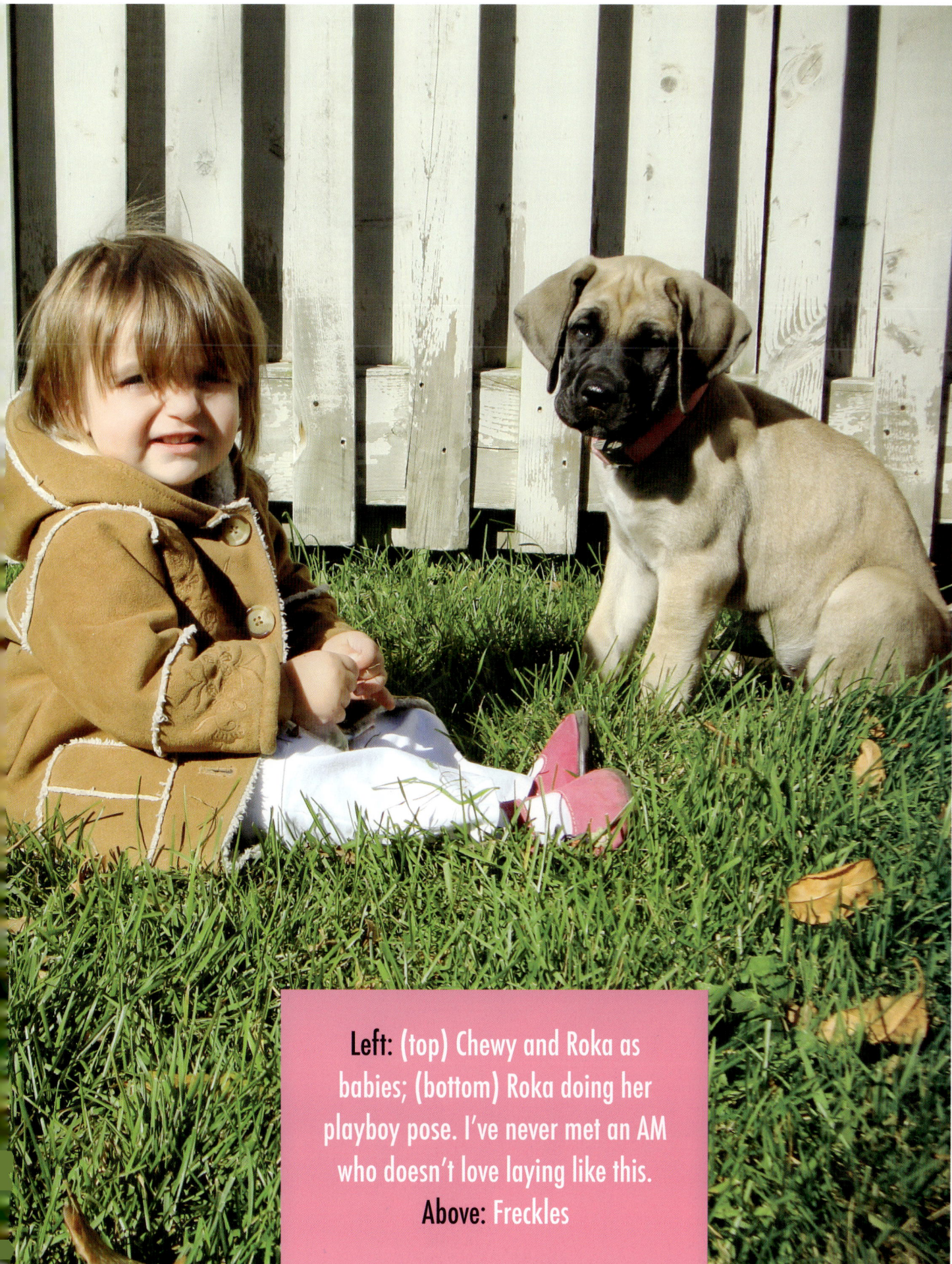

Left: (top) Chewy and Roka as babies; (bottom) Roka doing her playboy pose. I've never met an AM who doesn't love laying like this.
Above: Freckles

Left: Maddux
Right: (top to bottom)

Optimus Prime displaying a true characteristic of this breed, eating and sleeping at the same time!

Huxley and Samson on the cool tile

Hurley with his sister

Rose and Rocco

Training

One of the first things a potential American Mastiff adopter needs to know is how important it is to go through socialization and obedience training. This should be for any breed, actually, but it is extremely important with giant breeds. Let's be clear about why it is important: it's not because they are vicious by nature or born to be crazy, since they are certainly neither, yet they are so big that every little behavioral quirk can become a big deal to you and those around you.

For instance, when you go to a friend's house with a toy breed, like a Chihuahua, they may jump in excitement when you come in, run around, jump on your lap or asked to be petted. To the typical dog lover, this is no big deal, unless of course you are going out to eat and wearing your brand new designer dress, in which case, you should just stay in the car honking the horn incessantly until your friends come outside. For most of us, this is just a tiny dog being friendly and cute. Now let's imagine the same scenario with a 200-pound, 36" American Mastiff. This course of events turns into something resembling a lion-taming audition or an Olympic-caliber sport. This enthusiastic greeting might involve a calf-like creature careening into your knees, a baseball bat-sized tail whipping you, or a healthy dose of frothy slobber spread across your clothes all before you even get in the door. Once seated, you might even have an AM's bowling ball of a head landed right in your lap as he looks up at you adoringly. These two situations evoke very different reactions in house guests, but they are exactly the same to the dogs.

Let's say you love the mammoth-headed, motor-tailed, slobber-machine mountain lion that barks running around your house and being a total goofball. This is all good until you "want" them to listen. Whether it's behaving in the house, in public, or walking down the street, you have to have control over your dog. I can tell you right now, there isn't a person on this planet who is ready to be pulled down the street behind an American Mastiff. It would be like sledding in the snow without the sled, the snow, or even the soft winter coat one would usually wear. It would just be you, the pavement, and lots of Neosporin, unless you let your dog go, which would be even worse. If you spend some time watching the news or reading a newspaper, it can often seem like the general public and media are against big dogs. Even though the American Mastiff is not on any state or city 'banned breed' lists, like many of its unlucky cousins, it might not take much to prompt a change in the wrong direction. AMs are some of the friendliest, gentlest, sweetest dogs you will ever meet, but in the mind of a dog-fearing stranger, they could be perceived as huge, wild animals whose sole purpose in life is to eat little dogs and babies. While we know this is utter nonsense, these misguided impressions are further reason to emphasize socialization and obedience training with your AM. We certainly don't want our boys and girls to end up classified as part of any city's 'dangerous' group based solely on appearance, false perceptions or, more likely, bad owners. Before my first AM, I had a Pitbull-mix shelter dog who was amazingly gentle, and I've never met a dangerous or 'bad' bully-type breed dog...

ever! Still, uninformed government and media representatives have senselessly given some bully-type dogs a death sentence. I've been bitten by a Chihuahua and even a Chow-mix before, but never by a bully breed. You will never see Chihuahuas on the dangerous list because they are little. While this is unfortunate, it is also very true, so please, please, please train your dogs to be good citizens.

Although AMs are domesticated dogs like Poodles, Boxers or Beagles, having one as a family member is much like having a mountain lion, but without the wild nature. They are unbelievably strong and unrealistically huge, making them different than other dogs. Although most people have furkids they can control physically, not many people have that luxury with an American Mastiff. The good news is, you will rarely, if ever, need to control them physically. AMs, while big, are also very sweet and smart, so with the right training, they will happily listen to your every word. They have no idea they are bigger than most humans, and I don't see any reason for us to tell them

With Ludo, I started him in a puppy class with my trainer, Justine Oakwood, at Full Moon Dog Training. This allowed for early socialization and basic commands. At first, she would make housecalls with her Doberman until Ludo had his puppy shots. Then we moved to her class space. When I felt Ludo was safe to go into public, I took him everywhere with me. There are tons of places that will let you bring your AM puppy in to say, "hi". Some of the major ones that you should have near you are: pet supply chains, Lowes, and Home Depot. I like home improvement stores for human socialization since you aren't going to run into a bunch of other dogs there and pet supply chains are great when you want to focus on dog socialization. Parks and kids' playgrounds are important, too, as this will get them used to screaming, running, children and nature.

A minimum in training is to get through a basic obedience class, not just a puppy class. For those who wish to enhance their bond with

Barbara Bradford with Beuller, Ludo, Maximus, and Angus

Left: Vic and Gus sharing good eye contact.

Above: Ludo showing off is pottie skills!

Right: Keevah and big sister, Mya, the Saint Bernard. Having a well-trained adult dog aids in training, but continued human leadership is essential. Mya shows Keevah the ways of the beach.

their furkid and go further in training, there are more obedience classes to attend as well as training for therapy tests, rally work, and any other fun activity you would like to do with your dog. The only training I don't recommend is protection work. I say this because ALL American Mastiffs will naturally protect their family and property without any added training. There is also weight-pulling, which an AM would fair well at, however, it is extremely important to wait until they are done growing before pursuing this type of event training. Our boys and girls grow grow rapidly, but over a long period of time, not reaching adulthood until three or four years of age. Early training in weight-pulling could affect development and lead to joint problems later in life. Know your AM and his/her limits.

For those looking for a personal trainer in lieu of the big pet supply chain classes, feel free to talk to my trainer, and she can point you in the right direction. Justine is an amazing trainer and knows trainers with the same skillsets across the country. Her contact information is listed in the References section on page 211.

Grooming

Grooming is an important part of having a furkid of any species. Well-groomed animals are healthier, happier and definitely make everyone around them happier. There are a few key aspects I pay attention to when thinking about grooming. Ironically, they are the same aspects we think of as humans...lucky for us. In no particular order, they are hair, skin, teeth, nails, eyes, ears, odor. As you can see, these are all things we humans do naturally. Unfortunately for our American Mastiff kids, they do not possess thumbs so it's up to us, the extra-digit-folks, to do the hard work for them.

Hair:
This seems like an easy task for this short-hair breed, but it is more daunting than you may think. AMs have a dense undercoat that sheds tons if not taken care of on a regular basis. There are three products I whole heartedly endorse when it comes to brushing my boy, Ludo.

1. Rubber Horse Brush: this looks like a hard, rubber oval with jagged cutouts. Go outside with your pup and give her a rubdown with this brush. You might just find that a Pomeranian was hiding inside your kid's fur.

2. The Furminator: great product for getting JUST the undercoat, but can be a little tricky to master. It's possible to use it inside since the hair is more controlled.

3. Car shammy: these are great for just rubbing all over your dog to shine them up and get the loose hairs off.

Following a good routine of brushing and vacuuming will keep the shedding under control. AMs are considered to be average shedders.

Skin:
Some American Mastiffs have sensitive or dry skin, especially when they are puppies, but this is an easy fix. A good all natural shampoo/conditioner made for dogs is a good way to go. Diet can also affect dogs' skin. If you have a pup with really dry skin (which, fortunately, is rarely the case), there are over-the-counter and prescription solutions. I wouldn't worry too much about the occasional scratching though, assuming there are no bugs involved.

Teeth:
This has got to be one of the most important things you can do to improve the life of your furkid AND yours! Out of all the grooming tasks, teeth are often overlooked or dismissed due to the perceived complexity of brushing a dog's teeth. Good dental hygiene will prevent a number of diseases, bad breathe, and even financial stress. The five minutes of potential frustration between your furkid and you will prove to be worth every minute! Some dogs take naturally to teeth-brushing while others make it seem like the hardest thing on the planet. There are various training techniques that can help socialize your dog to having their teeth brushed, but I haven't had the patience to stick with any of them. Ludo is very social

Right: Ludo's pearly whites!

and tolerant of me touching his mouth, inside and out, but he is still no fan of getting his teeth brushed. Well, let me clarify, he LOVES licking the toothpaste, but just isn't a fan of sitting still while I brush his teeth. Here is my bulletproof and fun way of brushing Ludo's teeth that I'm sure will pay off for anyone who gives it a shot.

1. Buy dog toothpaste from your local pet supply store.

2. Go to your grocery store and buy the cheap four-pack of human tooth brushes.

3. Find some duct tape around the house (I know you have some).

This is all you need to ensure bright whites in your pup and more money in the bank! First, take the four toothbrushes and put them brush-side out, in a circular arrangement. Then duct tape around the stems so that you have created a four-sided human toothbrush. Next, take the dog toothpaste and put it on all four sides. Lastly, catch your furkid laying down and tired, or, if you are feeling frisky, do it while they are up running around. Just lift a lip flap and insert the brush. They will more than likely chew on it and try to lick off all the good stuff while you are brushing, but just keep brushing back and forth on the inside and outside of the teeth, ensuring you get the polar icecap-sized teeth in the back.

Doing this toothbrush dance with your dog once or twice a month (or even more, if you wish), along with a good diet and treats will keep your kid's chompers pearly white and super healthy. The third thing people always notice about Ludo is his Hollywood smile! First and second are his "small" stature, and "vicious" nature...sarcastically speaking, of course.

On another note, though, feeding a whole prey style raw diet minimizes the need for teeth-brushing. I still occasionally brush Ludo's teeth just to make myself feel better, but, in reality, the raw diet takes care of everything for me.

Nails:

Along with their giant-sized heads, legs, ears, teeth, neck, and feet, AMs have enormous toe nails as thick as a #2 pencil and as strong as iron. The easiest way for the humans is to pay someone else to do this daunting task, but the easiest thing for the dogs and our pockets is to socialize them to it being done at home. My personal favorite tool for the job is an industrial Dremel (the ones you find at your local tool supply store). They come in battery operated and plug-in versions. These are the *real* versions of the "Pedipaw" advertised on TV. The pedipaw is a great tool for smaller breeds, but it doesn't have the power necessary to grind down Mastiff-sized nails. Socializing your pup to this great tool is a slow process during which you let them gradually get used to it. This can be accomplished in steps over the course of a week or so: let them hear it, let them feel it, do one nail, do a couple of nails, do more nails, and so on. Be sure to use positive reinforcement and load up on treats along the way!

Ludo is still not a huge fan of getting his nails done, but he does tolerate it to an extent. I like to wait until he is tired and passed out on the floor, just to make it easier on myself.

The other option is to buy extra large and strong traditional dog nail clippers. This is certainly a faster and cheaper way to cut their nails. I have decided against traditional clippers for Ludo not only because I don't trust myself to not cut the nail quick, but also because the nails are quite sharp after clipping. This can be improved by using a good file afterwards, but I just find the dremel works better for me. It really comes down to personal preference and skill levels using both tools.

A quick note on cutting the quick: it does cause temporary pain to your pet, which none of us like, and there is a good amount of blood that will ooze out. While there is nothing we can do to prevent the pain portion, there is a magical solution to stop the bleeding immediately. Cornstartch is the magical medicinal tool of

French tips, please!

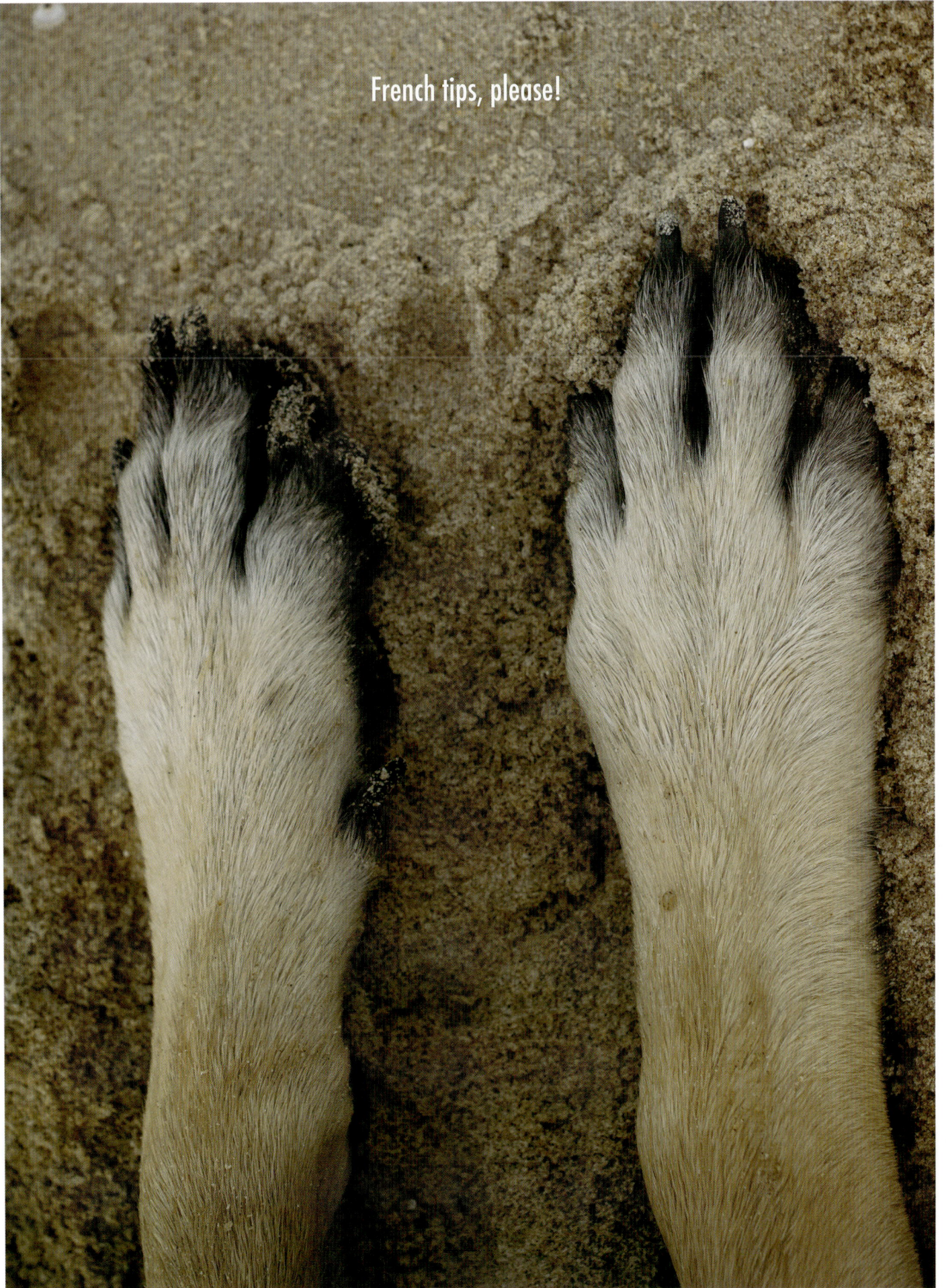

choice for stopping the bleeding. Veterinarians use a fancier named version (stypic powder), but it's all mainly cornstarch, in my opinion. For those do-it-yourselfers at home, this method works on humans, too. I've used cornstarch many times to stop my cuts and pokes from bleeding.

Eyes:

This is an easy one! Our big furkids have droopier eyes than most dogs so they have eye mucus (rheum or "eye boogers"), typically on a daily basis. It's nothing crazy or obscene, but it's something that should be taken care of. We always want our boys and girls to look their best, plus I'm sure they don't want goop going back into their eye and getting in the way of seeing that TREAT on the floor! The solution is easy... just wipe and go.

Ears:

Besides being extremely adorable and fun to play with, American Mastiff ears can also play host to bacteria and bugs. This applies to all dogs and cats, but, in our case, we have a bigger surface to cover. The best way to take care of your pup's ears are to look in them, smell them, and wipe them out. Once you know what your pup's ears are supposed to smell and look like, then if you notice an odd odor or visual deviation, you'll know something is up. A good way to keep your pup's ears clean and fun for all is to occasionally wipe them out. I personally use a 25/75 ratio home-made mix of apple cider vinegar and water, but there are also pre-packaged solutions available. I soak a cotton ball into this mixture and squeeze out the excess liquid. Wiping the inside of the ear and a little into the canal will prevent bacteria from growing in the ears. Be sure you don't get any liquid down into the canal, though; a good moist wipe inside the ear will do the job.

Odor:

The last item on my personal grooming list is odor. To some people this means the typical "dog smell", to others it means rolling in a skunk or playing in the mud. However we classify odor or determine what level is acceptable to us, there are several ways to improve it. Dozens of fragrance sprays, waterless shampoos, oils, and all natural options are available at your local pet supply store. Personally, I would only consider using something more natural, without a harsh or alcohol-based formula, to ensure it doesn't cause dry skin or unnecessary scratching. These products are, of course, outside of bathing which should be done when needed. Again, this is a personal preference amongst all dog owners. I lean more towards the "less is more" side of bathing, typically giving Ludo a bath a handful of times per year unless he gets into something stinky. Rest assured, however, there is no wrong answer as long as you ensure your dog's skin is staying moisturized.

Kona enjoying some deer for dinner

Diet and Nutrition

A topic that is always at the top of a new AM's, or any puppy's, owner's mind is, "what do I feed my newest family member to ensure I'm doing right by them?" This is never an easy question to answer since there are so many different views on canine diets out there in the virtual world, but the best thing to do is to learn from others' mistakes, as well as from their vast knowledge and research. Many breeders, scholars and owners have spent countless hours, days, weeks, and even months, studying ingredients and nutritional values, and even conducting trial and error testing to determine which foods are best for their dogs and for the breed as a whole.

With our big boys and girls, nutrition plays a vital role in their growth and overall health. American Mastiffs grow at such a fast rate that it is up to us, their parents, to ensure we fulfill their dietary needs. It's very easy to go to the grocery store and buy a 50 pound bag of large breed puppy food for $15.00 and be done with it. What we might fail to realize at the time is the long-term effect of this strategy, not only on budget but also on our dogs' health. While we might save some money up front by opting for cheap kibble, we also may end up paying 100 times what we've saved in veterinary bills due to poor nutrition or growth problems associated with the inappropriate nutritional values contained in inferior dog food.

My personal opinion, along with thousands of other dog owners, from toy breeds to giants, is that the best diet for our furry friends is the one nature intended, raw whole prey. There is not enough room in this book to include all the reasons to feed a whole prey style raw diet, but I will provide a little insight from all my research and the research of others. First, let me mention that I fed dry kibble to my boy, Ludo for the first 17 months of his life. I knew of the existence of the raw fed diet, but never took the time to research it and always assumed it would be way more expensive and time consuming. My dog trainer, Justine Oakwood, owner of Full Moon Dog Training, feeds both her therapy Doberman and shelter dog a whole prey style raw diet and encourages others to research it. At the time, Ludo was doing well on his super premium kibble and I never took the time to research raw. After traveling the country meeting other AM owners, I met Rachel Lamory and her two furkids, Ti and Kingston.

Rachel mentioned that both of her boys are raw fed, and it piqued my curiousity again. By this time, however, Ludo wasn't a hundred percent on his super premium food. He was off and on with having loose stools, and he would literally fertilize the yard with the amount of poop he would download every day. After getting back from my trip, I began to do more research on this raw diet, searching the internet, joining online groups, and, more importantly, speaking with experienced people I knew personally for insight. I contacted Justine and Rachel and talked with them about it for a week or two, while doing the web surfing. I began to realize not only did I "want" to start feeding raw, but I "needed" to!

Now came the hard part of figuring out how I could possibly afford such a dramatic change in diet. So what I did was calculated how much money I was spending in kibble to feed three dogs. Then I determined how many pounds I would have to feed the boys per day, and per month. Then, based on what others can get

Right: Lurch (R.I.P.) enjoying a raw, meaty bone as a treat in the backyard (even though he was on a kibble diet). Lurch loved to hang out in his yard. I hung a wind chime with his name on it the day he passed away so he would always be out there with me.

meat for, based those pounds on a price at an average of $1.00/lb, thus giving me an estimate of monthly spending. Comparing the two costs, kibble versus raw, they were the same! This was an awesome surprise for me and my wallet. Plus, the best thing about it in terms of price is during hunting season and sales, you can save a ton of money. I don't personally hunt or promote the killing of animals for sport, but for my dogs' sake, I certainly won't turn down meat derived by hunting. That takes care of the money worries associated with feeding a raw diet, so let's look at the health benefits.

When we initially think about feeding our furkids raw food, a bunch of thoughts run through our heads like they'll choke on bones, or bones will splinter in their bellies, and what about parasites and diseases found in raw meat? Good news... dogs are NOT humans, and therefore all of these concerns are void. Bones only splinter when cooked. Never give your dogs cooked bones. On the other hand, raw bones from all animals are great for them and are easily digested, as dogs have specialized stomachs built for the consumption of bones. The only bones to stay away from are the leg bones of strong four legged animals, [i.e. cows, deer, goat, etc]. because they are so strong and hard that they can chip and even break teeth. All other bones are fair game. With parasites and diseases, again, dogs are better equipped to deal with these than are humans. The acids in a dog's stomach takes care of all kinds of nasty stuff a dog decides to eat.

The things we have to consider when choosing between kibble and feeding a whole prey style raw diet are as follows:

1. Kibble is processed and loaded with

preservatives, and the meat source is often unclear, as opposed to raw, which is an all natural source much like a dog would find in the wild.

2. Kibble is loaded with grain (except grain free), veggies, and fruit versus raw which is 100% meat source, bone, and organs. This is very important since dogs are strictly carnivores and never, ever need grains, veggies or fruits. These are all items that are healthy for human consumption (which is how kibble campaigns are able to connect with us).

3. A dog's DNA is around 99% identical to the wolf, who never eats kibble. Even more important, the digestive system of a dog is 100% identical to that of a wolf, which means they are made to eat the same diet as a wild wolf.

4. Don't buy into your vet's propaganda on how a dog should eat kibble. You have to remember, they are very knowledgable in fixing your dog should they become injured, but have very little real education on diet. In fact, the education they do receive is typically given by kibble-producing companies.

5. Kibble has only been around for about a half a century. So how have dogs survived for all these years without the creation of kibble? Easy... a raw diet, and at times scraps from their humans. Just ask the oldest member of your extended family what they fed their dogs, and you may be surprised by their answer.

Now for the all important information on how you feed a whole prey style raw diet. It's easy! The general rule is to feed 2-3% of your dog's ideal adult body weight per day. For my AM, that's about 3-5 pounds a day. The make up of your meals should be 80% meat, 10% bone, and 10% organs. This doesn't have to be as strict as it sounds, nor does it all have to be in one meal. Dogs, like wolves, adapt to all kinds of eating patterns and habits, based on what's available. These percentages are a general rule that will provide a technically "balanced" meal. There are numerous ways you can feed them. Also, product-wise, they can eat literally any prey-style animal, poultry, beef, pork, deer, rodents, rabbits, fish. The best thing to do is to go online and do your research. There are tons of resources to provide guidance along the way. From my personal experience so far in feeding raw to my boys, they are super healthy and they have great muscle tone, great balanced energy levels, great coats, and great poops! Yes, that's right, their poop is AMAZING! Ludo has gone from using the bathroom a few times a day, some solid, some loose, to literally going once or twice and being firm and incredibly small. If I didn't know any better, I would think a poodle was pooping in my backyard. Not to mention the fact that the dogs absolutely love it! They are so much happier to eat raw food versus their kibble. You can just tell that they are built to tear through their food as they prance around the yard with their "catch" in their mouth. They couldn't be happier!

Now I know that not everyone will choose to feed their dogs a whole prey style raw diet for various reasons, and it is not my intention to sway anyone else's decision or to be judgmental. There are a number of kibble options out there to choose from that fall in the correct ranges of nutritional values as well as price points for our big boys and girls. I have listed a variety of kibble (in no particular order) for your new

puppy as well as once they become adults that many other AM owners feed their furkids.

Holisitc Select
Taste of the Wild
Blue Buffalo
Wellness
Nature's Domain
Exclusive
Fromm's
Precise
Nutri-Source
Pure Vita
Planet Oragnics
Nature's Logic
Wysong
Honest Kitchen

I still encourage everyone to do a little research on their own simply for the sake of understanding why and how these foods stack up against other brands and against raw. I have read enough about dog food, along with some of my American Mastiff Forum family members, to receive an imaginary Doctorate in Canine Nutrition. As a pretend doctor of doggie nutrition, I can say it all comes down to doing what's right for you and your newest family member. Whether you feed raw food, or a good quality kibble, ensure your furkid lives the healthiest life possible, as I can assure you they will give you the happiest life possible every time they lay their head in your lap and look at you.

Team Bradford, like a pride of lions on the plain

Treat choice is as equally important as picking the right food for your pup. There are hundreds if not thousands of treat options out there for your furkid. Just go to the local animal supply store and look at the aisles upon isles of doggie snacks, all stating to be better than the next. As with kibble, you must read the labels and determine the quality of a treat product using your new knowledge. If the treats have too high of a protein or calcium/phosphorus content, stay away while your pup grows. If the list presents a bunch of grains and unrecognizable ingredients, chances are it is an inferior product. From my standpoint, I choose only treats that have a handful of ingredients or less, and only list things I am familiar with. My treat of choice for my raw fed boys is freeze-dried liver. While it can be quite pricey, I buy the big tub and it lasts me a while. There is only one ingredient in freeze-dried liver, you guessed it, liver! That is natures best treat in my opinion. Other great options include homemade treats like Peanut Butter Pumpkin Biscuits (listed on the AMfamilyforum), Hemalayan Yack Cheese, and of course anything truly natural, [i.e. one ingredient meat source]. For the freeze dried liver, I use Stewart's Pro-Treat 21 oz tub from Amazon.com.

Feeding a raw diet is like being on safari or watching a live episode from the National Geographic Channel. There is nothing like seeing your dog eat in the way of his ancestors.

Ludo devours a five-pound chicken

Health Issues

While the American Mastiff is generally one of the healthiest giant breed dogs, they are still susceptible to certain size-related health issues and to diseases that affect all dogs.

Bloat:
Technically referred to as "gastric volvulus" or "gastric torsion", bloat is a deadly turning of the stomach prevalent in all deep-chested breeds. Prevention is aided by limited activity around feedings, but there are no bulletproof measures other than surgery. Proper eating, and exercise regimes will help prevent bloat greatly. Please do more research on bloat if considering ANY deep chested breed, such as a Boxer, Bulldog, Mastiff, Doberman, German Shepherd or Great Dane.

Hip and elbow dysplasia:
Although assumed by many to be solely a genetic issue, dysplasia can also be brought on by poor care during growth. There are genetic traits which can lead to pups having dysplasia, but the AMBC screens their breeding stock for such defects to prevent any genetic prevalence. As an AM owner, the more important factors to focus on when considering dysplasia are proper nutrition levels and exercise limitations during growth periods. Mastiff puppies should never be allowed to jump off anything high or to run across slippery surfaces where they might lose traction. Simple preventative measures can help ensure your AM grows up to be a big, strong dog that's as healthy as an ox.

Cancer:
Cancer is seen more now in all dogs, and American Mastiffs are no exception. This is the hardest diseases to deal with and predict, although theories abound on the canine cancer linkage. With these bigger guys and girls, bone cancer seems to be seen the most. Recent theories on bone cancer include genetics as well as the presence of stress fractures in pups. This goes back to not allowing your pup to jump off anything high or put too much stress on joints and bones during the first 2 years of growth.

All in all, American Mastiffs are very hardy and healthy dogs with the typical health issues related to giant or deep-chested breeds. The good news is, these things can "somewhat" be prevented and controlled with proper nutrition and exercise from day one through the rest of their lives, with the average AM living to be 10-12 years of age. The longest living American Mastiff on record was, Sandy, a female from Flying W Farms who was 16 years of age.

Left: Ludo wanted to stop and take a picture in front of his favorite word during our road trip.

As responsible AM guardians, it is up to us to do what is best for our furkids' health. Keep your dogs healthy and they will return the favor.

Health Insurance:

There are generally two two camps when it comes to canine health insurance: those who think it's necessary, and those who think it's pointless. Both sides have valid points and many people from both groups have amazing success stories.

The necessity crowd believe that insurance offers peace of mind, and that it will pay for itself many times over if anything serious were to happen to ever happen to their furkid.

The other side believes they are better off to put the money they would have spent on monthly insurance premiums into a separate bank account for their dog (almost like a college fund). This method allows parents to keep the money if the fund is never needed, but it also ensures the funds are there when they are needed most.

Both of these plans are practical and I believe the best one is whichever makes the guardians feel more comfortable. What I don't advocate is leaving things to chance, since this can often result in heartbreaking and even life-threatening consequences. Personally, I choose to have the insurance. I would love to be able to keep some money in a special account just for Ludo, but I am so much more comfortable knowing I have an "endless" supply of money at my fingertips if needed (through the insurance company). This method paid off greatly in my case. Ludo needed a surgery on his elbow which cost $3000, and at that point I had only put in around $400 on the insurance policy. It would have been much more difficult financially to have the procedure done if I didn't have the health coverage in place. In my case, it has already paid for itself. I wish I could say the opposite, since my boy Ludo would have never had to go through treatment and recovery, but it's nice to know the money is there.

I use Trupanion for Ludo. Out of all the pet insurance companies I've researched, they had the best coverage and reimbursement plans, including dysplasia (which many companies do NOT cover). The key is to sign up as soon as

you bring your pup home to ensure everything under the sun is covered. If an issue is deemed to be present before the health coverage started, it is not covered (prior to eight weeks old doesn't count). This is true for most pet insurance companies.

Supplements:

On top of a healthy diet and good treats, many AM guardians also give their pooches supplements. Some people use a lot, some people, none. I personally use Connectin, a joint support powder, 100% natural Alaskan Salmon Oil for a healthy heart and coat, and Plaque-off, a seaweed mix that creates natural plaque fighting saliva. Every morning after the boys eat their whole chicken, beef hearts, or whatever is on the menu, they are treated with a bowl of salmon oil, connectin powder, plaque-off, and local honey mixed together into a green goo. If you ask them, it is to die for! It helps with joint stiffness, a good shiny, soft coat, white teeth, and hayfever protection. I know it may seem like a lot, but in reality, it takes me less than two minutes to get their food ready, and another minute to get their green goo put together (which I do while they are eating outside). This is our morning routine, or what I like to call "getting the kids ready for school".

Above: Kieren and Daegan make great pillows.
Right: Ludo is a practicing Doctor, and specializes in Cardiology, as he heels the hearts of many...

A special note about parasite protection. While there are a lot of products on the market to prevent parasite infections (heartworm, fleas, ticks), there are also all natural ways to protect our furkids without exposing them to toxins. For fleas, ticks, and flying insects I use an all natural Cedar Spray from GreenBug. com. This products works great on dogs AND humans!

For heartworm, I unfortunately haven't found any non-toxic solution, but I do suppliment the medication with Milk Thistle. This herbal rememdy helps detoxify the liver. I give it to the dogs for a few days after using Heartguard+.

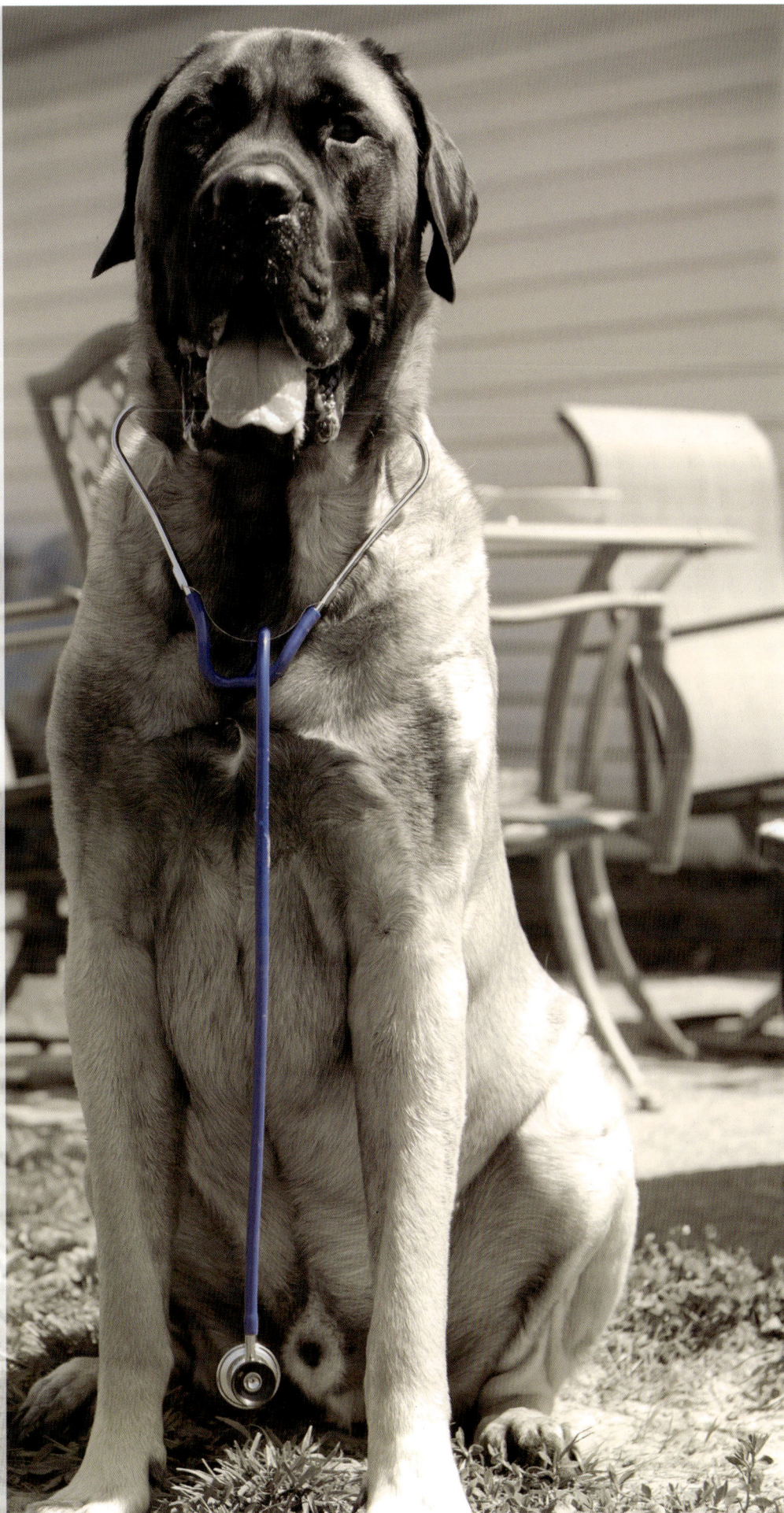

Toys!

Ah yes, the most fun part about being a dog and a dog parent...buying all the cool toys you can afford in an effort to watch your furkid prance in delight. For anyone who has owned a dog before, you know how dog toys can be the money pit of your existence. Now add to that a dog with the mouth of a grizzly bear and you are really taking a risk with every purchase from your local pet store. My goal here is to inform you of what has worked and failed miserably for me and for other Mastiff owners from around the country. From this list you can decide which ones you want to try. You may strike it rich with some of them and throw others away after two hours of pure destruction...you just never know and every dog is different.

Here are a list of suggested "tried and true" toys thanks to our AM Community:

LynnsTugToyz (facebook.com/LynnsTugToyz)
Kong Wubba (or other Kong toys)
Nyalabone
Jolly Ball
Indestructaball
Moose antlers
Deer antlers
Rough Toys
Metal-Free Tires
Ropes
Empty plastic bottles
Stuffing Free Toys
Gummy Nylabones (in the freezer for teething)

To this day, Ludo still has (and chews on) his XLarge Nylabone that looks like a leg bone.

He gone through antlers (which do last a while in moderation), and all the kong toys (within days if not hours), but his Nylabone still remains intact and a fan favorite along with his real leg bones. The plus side to antlers, is they are free if you know a hunter who doesn't keep the rack.

He also loves the XXXXXL rope toy I bought at Tractor Supply. They tend to last a long time as well considering their size, and they are cheap enough to buy every six months or so when they wear out.

All I can say, is GOOD LUCK! All AMs are different; player, chewer, or destroyer. Just base your toy selections on what category your pup ends up falling under. This will save you tons of money while giving your dog happy days in the yard and house.

Most recently, I have found that 100% rubber tires are a great addition to the backyard. I scored a riding lawn mower tire for free and Ludo loves carrying it in his mouth. Yes, these guys can do that! Ludo could carry a car tire in his mouth if he wanted to. If you find free tires, just make sure they don't have metal built into them or any toxic substances on the outside.

Right: As a puppy, Ludo loved his Pawtracks tire. Now he plays with real tires from a riding lawnmower.

Ludo's Favorites: Riding lawnmower tire, Kong Wubba, and Jolly Ball

These guys and girls love, love, LOVE earthy items. A lot of American Mastiffs are known to be "grazers" as they constantly eat and chew Mother Nature's treats like grass, weeds, leaves, sticks, and sometimes even rocks! Common sense prevails when deciding what to allow your AM to chew on. Establishing a consistant "drop-it" command is essential with these big kids. I've found that using treats much tastier than what's in their mouth is the best method. A good practice is to do this throughout the day, not just when they have a squirrel in their mouth. An Alpha leader should be able to open their AM's mouth without too much fuss in special cases, but I don't recommend it for strangers or kids. Ludo is stubborn if he has something really tasty, but I make it a point to ALWAYS win. I personally like to keep his "stick" play to limbs, like the one to the left. Smaller sticks break too easily and if ingested the wrong way can cause trouble...just not worth the risk to me.

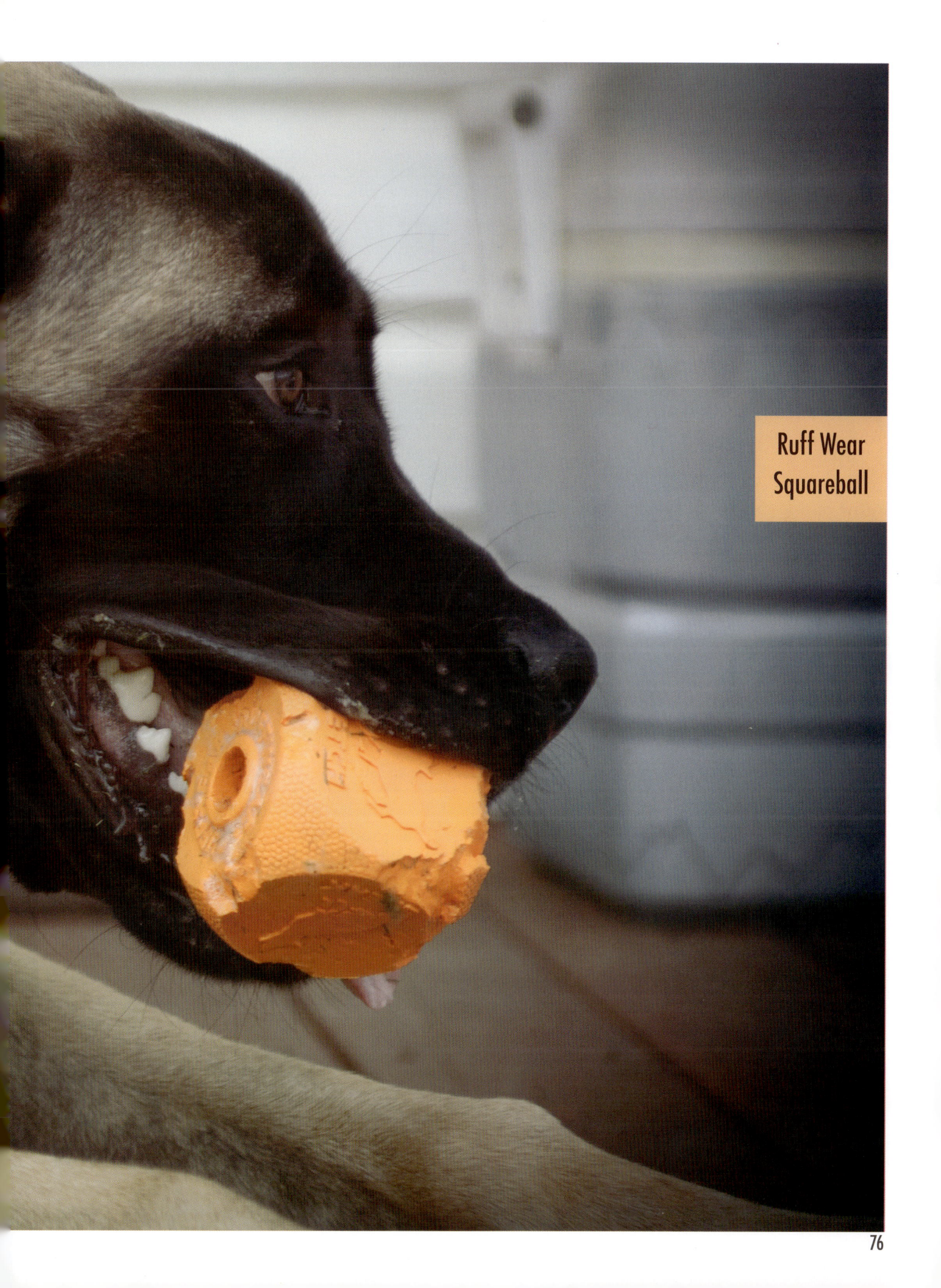

Ruff Wear
Squareball

Accessories

In the modern world, even the most rugged pet owner wants to reflect some sort of persona in their furkids' fashion accessories. The good AND bad news about your child being an American Mastiff is you will be buying tons of collars as your pup grows. At the rate AMs grow during the first couple of years, they will most likely outgrow a collar before it even has a chance to get dirty. Let's take a look at what to expect with collars and leashes.

Leashes

There is really only one leash you will ever need in life, and that is a leather one. A good leather leash that you have softened up with polishing oils will last a lifetime. Besides lifespan, a leather leash provides the best strength and comfort for you and your dog. Nylon leashes, while more stylish, can leave your hands burnt, which will inevitabley make you frustrated (something that is not good when it comes to training and being with your furkid).

If you don't go the leather route, there are other styles that are very durable, but just be prepared for the burn.

Collars

AM pups are already in a small-medium sized collar at eight weeks when they go home. This collar will only last a short time, so be on the lookout for that perfect collar that will compliment your pup. Over the time that I've had Ludo (who is currently 18 months old), we've gone through five collars. I admit one or two of them were for holiday spirit, but, none the less, you will at least need three.

The bad news with collars and our big kids is that around the 12-24 month mark, they may no longer fit into ANY commercial collars sold at the big box pet supply stores. The largest size you will typically find in stores are 26-28 inches. Yes, your little boy or girl will not be able to fit in this size, in most cases.

Right: Shayna
Below: Kona the pirate! It turns out that the hat was a huge hit...Kona loved wearing it.

The good news is we now have an American Mastiff team member that produces their very own line of collars and leashes for giant breeds! They also cater to smaller breed sizes if you have other furkids in the house that want to be as stylish as their big brother or sister. The company's name is LIVE, LIFE, LARGE, and they can be found on Facebook as well as the reference section of this book. Their motto is: At Live, Life, Large, our original intent was to custom make what could not be found in the stores..."cute" collars for the larger breed dogs. We have rapidly expanded to collars and leashes in four sizes, "poo poo pouches" and horse halters.

Visit them at www.livelifelargecollars.com.

Don't get me wrong, there are other online resources that cater to giant breed collars and accessories, but this particular business is in "our" family and sell their products at a much more reasonable price point, about half that of the competition. Ludo currently wears his black and red paw print collar from LIVE, LIFE, LARGE as it matches his Atlanta Falcons jersey. He's a southern boy!

Training Collars

Sometimes training collars play an integral part of a dog's training program. Not all dogs will need a training style collar, but with these big kids, I have found training collars a necessity at some point or another. There are many styles out there, but the two I like most are the typical chain style collar that hangs loosely on the neck until a correction is needed. The other is the prong collar, which is more like a mother dog nipping their puppy. These collars look scary and mean, but I assure you, they are not. Proper fit is very important as well as proper use in correcting your furkid with any collar type. With prong collars, in particular, I have found that the cheaper ones are a lot sharper and I am not comfortable putting them on my dogs. Spend the extra money and get a good, high quality brand with smooth rounded tips that you can comfortably rub and poke into your hand. The goal is correction/attention, not pain. Pain should never be used as a training tool. Startle, snap to attention, or surprise, but please don't use pain or abuse. This will only break your bond with your dog and undermine trust, in my opinion.

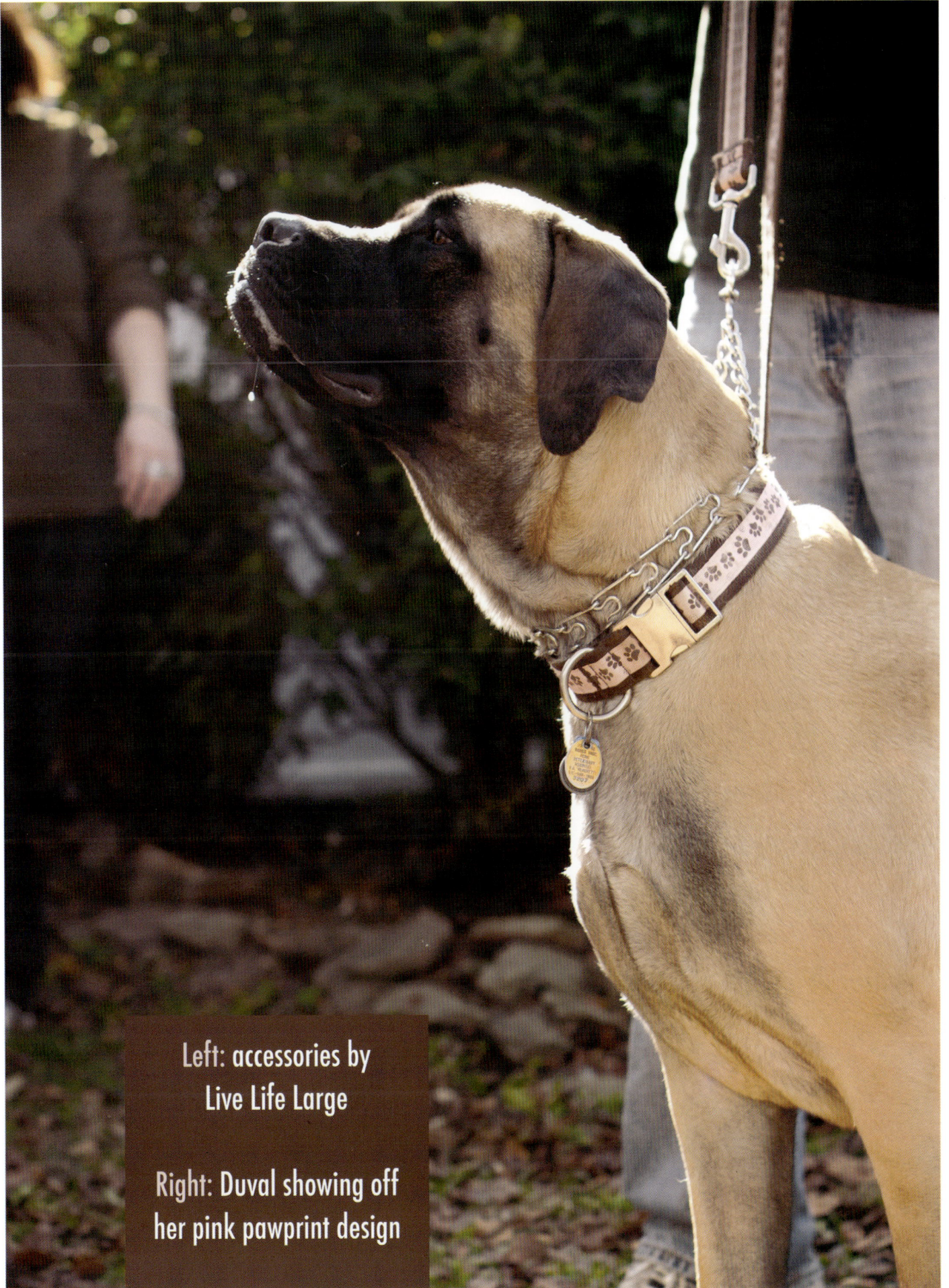

Left: accessories by
Live Life Large

Right: Duval showing off
her pink pawprint design

Left: Moomba, retired female from Orion Farms

Right: Atlas

Bueller sporting his Live Life
Large striped collar

Holidays are great times to show off our AMs and their festive spirits. Just because we don't have five-pound Chihuahuas doesn't mean we can't play dress-up with our furkids, too. In fact, the smaller the accessory the funnier our giants look!

Left: Winnifred doing some Halloween howling and pumpkin "carving"

Right: Savannah's Saint. Patty's day parade. Dano and Tiffany White with Ludo (six months old). It's safe to say that Ludo got more attention and photo ops than the actual parade, which is the second largest in the nation next to Boston. * Green beer, giant dog... GOOD TIMES!

Ludo and his sister-in-law, Chloe, excited about Santa

Left: Ludo loves his Swamp Cooler Vest from RuffWear. This is the perfect accessory for hot days as it keeps these big guys cool and their internal temperature down.

Above: A plastic kiddie pool is another summertime option.

Right: Rufus and Ludo tried out for Santa's team this year. He chose Rudolph again!?! How disappointing!

The AMBC

The AMBC, or American Mastiff Breeder's Council, is the heart and soul of this amazing breed. It was established by the original creators of the American Mastiff at Flying W Farms in an effort to maintain integrity with the breed and to protect it from things such as overpopulation, poor breeding standards, and the typical issues seen in a lot of the more popular breeds in America. We are in an unfortunate society where puppy mills pop up everyday, causing an endless amount of animals to suffer all in the name of money. What the American Mastiff community has done with this breed is remarkable and should be the staple in all breeding programs across the globe. In a world full of animal shelters that are forced to put down animals every day, it's nice to see a council that's out to reverse this unfortunate situation of overpopulation.

The AMBC monitors all American Mastiff offspring as they grow. This is largely facilitated by the wonderful lines of communication between the AMBC approved breeders and their carefully screened owners. The breeders literally become an extended part of your family. As a new AM owner, you will want to brag about your new furkid as well as send pictures, ask questions, and inevitabley ask for another furball of sunshine. Being such a close-knit community, it is very rare that an American Mastiff is seen in a shelter or a bad situation. Though it does seldom happen, our AM families unite and take care of the situation immediately, through means of volunteering, rescue, transportation, fostering and funding. For these reasons and more, you will never see an overpopulation of AMs, nor will you see them in shelters, junkyards, on chains, or for sale in parking lots and flea markets. I cannot express enough how much I appreciate the AMBC and all they do for animals. I, personally, am a huge animal rights advocate and always put animals above myself in every scenario, even to the point that I am a vegetarian. The AMBC is everything that I look for in a breeder, community, and family.

Currently there are 10 breeders approved by the AMBC and they can be found on their website, along with information and links to useful information regarding the breed.

All the AMBC breeders are not recognized in this book through imagery (due to my inability to visit them all), but they are all equally fantastic and as a potential American Mastiff parent, you will be in great hands with any of the 10. All breeders have personal websites associated with their breeding programs that provide you with great information and contact details. I strongly suggest reaching out to the breeders in your area to schedule a time to visit them to meet their fantastic furkids and see how wonderful their breeding program really is. Some breeders even offer open farm days during the warmer months where you can visit and see their breeding stock along with pups that have come from their program's past. This allows you to meet not only the breeders' dogs, but also other owners who were once in your shoes. The amount of information to be gained from these open farm days is immeasurable.

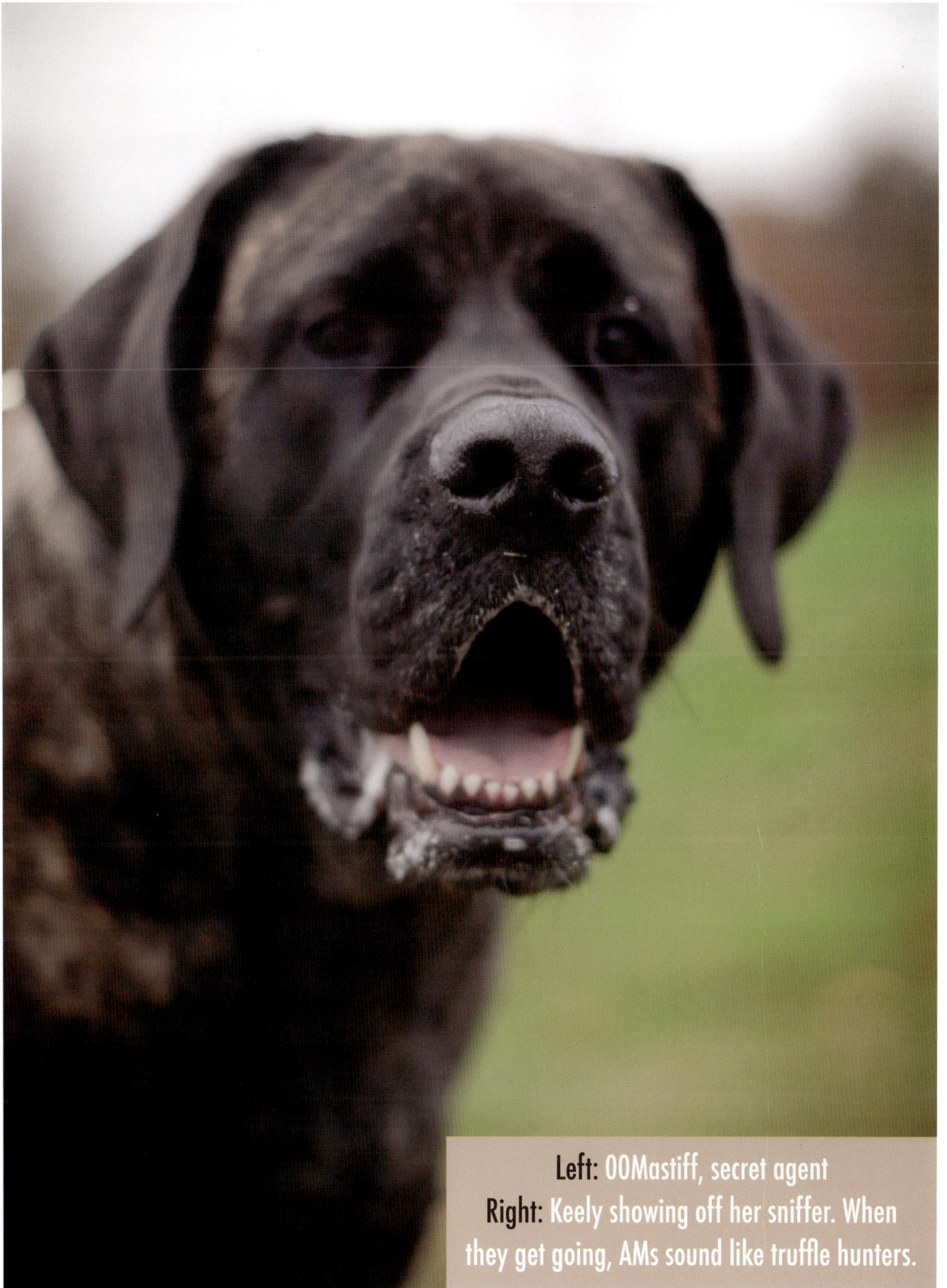

Left: 00Mastiff, secret agent
Right: Keely showing off her sniffer. When they get going, AMs sound like truffle hunters.

Left: Gryphon
Right: Achilles

American Mastiffs typically love cruising the beach and some even venture into the ocean. The hard part is finding dog-friendly beaches these days.

Left: Vayda Right: Ludo

Brother and sister saying, "Hi again!" since they left their litter six months earlier

Rocco is the guardian of the farm. He enjoys the beautiful New York fall.

My Boy, Ludo

My journey with the American Mastiff began in Hawaii. My ex-wife and I were stationed at Hickam AFB on the island of Oahu. I had just finished my enlistment and she was a career airman. We received orders to Georgia and wanted to bring a new family member into our lives. I grew up with dogs and can't see living my life without man's best friend and she grew up with cats and the occasional dog, but was on board with adding a furry member to our family...with the caveat we get a cat in the future as well.

Growing up around dogs and being a volunteer at the Humane Society, I have seen hundreds of breeds, and learned about plenty more on the internet and in books. No matter my environment, I always gravitated more towards the bully-type breeds in a pack. Even at the humane society, the Pitbull mixes and other bully type breeds were often neglected and gained much of my attention. In fact, I was so in love with them that I adopted a Pitbull-mix while stationed in Germany as a single Staff Sergeant. He lived with me until I deployed and was no longer able to take care of him. I adopted him out to a family with a stay-at-home family member and kids. It was a tough decision for me, but definitely the best thing for the dog.

With it being time to choose a breed to become our newest family member, the list was narrowed down to two breeds, the American Bulldog and the Pitbull. I attended a couple of American Bulldog shows to meet some in person and fell in love. They were amazing dogs with great temperaments and a beautiful smile. The problem lay in the new laws I soon began to research online. I learned while living in Europe that certain dog breeds were not permitted to enter Germany and with this knowledge decided to dig a little deeper into dog breed bans in general. What I found blew my mind. Military bases were now beginning to regulate dog breeds by restricting bully breeds from living on base. With this new information and the future moves of my family in the Air Force, I couldn't bring in a new family member knowing that I may have to adopt them out once again.

The new breed search began. I started researching bully-type breeds with sweet temperaments that were good with kids as well as other animals. I wanted a dog that was relatively "bomb-proof" and could work towards being a therapy dog for kids and veterans. My mother was going through a separation at the time and was also looking for a fuzzy companion, so I was doing combined searches for her and myself. She had recently lost her Great Dane and wanted something similar without the incredibley short life span. Her Dane had been adopted through a Great Dane rescue in Virginia and lived until she was five years old. While searching giant breeds as well as breeds fitting my criteria, Mastiffs continually popped up. My mother was not a big fan of the drool, nor were my ex-wife and I. I had abandoned hope on any Mastiff breed with the majority of them being heavy droolers until, like magic, the American Mastiff showed up. I began to read all the information I could

find on them and decided this would be the PERFECT breed to fill the void of my mother's passed Great Dane. I continued to look into them and the more I learned, the more I wanted one for myself. My mother ended up rescuing a Pitbull-mix and I decided I wanted to meet an American Mastiff! It couldn't have worked out better, as she didn't have to worry about breed bans, and I found my future fur-kid.

Through the internet, I found a website that referred to an American Mastiff Breeder Council. This was a site dedicated to informing everyone on the breed, listing the approved breeders, and giving dog lovers a look into the life of an AM. I contacted one of the breeders and set up a date to come out and meet them. This breeder was Kerry at Lazy M Mastiffs in MA. At this time we had already moved to Georgia and I took a flight to meet Kerry. She was amazing, and her dogs were impressive, to say the least. I immediately got on her waiting list and soon welcomed my first AM, Lurch, to the family.

My first experience raising an American Mastiff puppy was great! Lurch was the easiest puppy to housetrain and learned boundaries very quickly. Outside of whining in his crate at night, he was a total angel. I was able to enjoy six wonderful months with my fur-kid before he crossed the "Rainbow Bridge" due to some unknown illness. One day he started limping and getting a fever, then he eventually couldn't stand up on his own. Lurch spent two weeks in the personal care of his veterinarian being treated for everything they could possibly think of, but the treatment failed and he slipped away at 7:30 in the morning, right before my birthday party. I was devastated! It took a long time for me to get through the process of losing my boy. Kerry, the breeder, was so supportive through the entire process and aided in the healing. The mystery behind Lurch's passing was the most frustrating part. I wanted to know if I did something wrong, if he was bit by a snake in the yard, if he picked up an infection, or if it was something genetic. My vet could not give an answer to this question, but assured me there was nothing I could have done differently.

I still miss Lurch, but he played such a huge role in my life that I can still feel him in everything I do with my current AM Ludo. Lurch solidified my predictions on how awesome this breed is, and I am forever thankful to him and Kerry for sharing in those six months with me.

With the loss of Lurch, I had to personally work through the grieving process before even considering bringing another furkid into my life. After six months, I was ready to fill the empty space Lurch left in my heart. I reached out to a few breeders with my story and the feedback was outstanding. The breeders were already aware of my story from reading posts on the AMFamily forum and were more than eager to put me at the top of the waiting list for their next breeding...this blew my mind. I decided to go with the Ware family at Orion Farms in Maryland. The timing of their breeding schedule worked perfect with when I was ready to bring home a new bundle of joy. Before bringing Ludo home, I was able to go to an open house when the puppies were about five weeks old. Along with a couple of my friends, Colleen and Josh, I enjoyed a day full of fluffy little pups playing in the yard, licking faces, and sleeping in laps. With 11 pups running around, I had no idea which one would be coming home with me in a couple more weeks, and I didn't care because they were all precious. The way Orion does their program is amazing, but for those potential parents who like the idea of "picking" their puppy based on the way they looked at them, or the first one to walk up and say hi, you are in for a surprise. The Ware family takes great pride in placing the right pup with the appropriate family. In doing so, they wait the full seven or eight weeks to see how the personality of each pup develops then weighs these traits against the needs and situations of the potential families. This process does two things; it ensures the family will be happy with their new furkid for the life of their relationship, and, more importantly, places the pup in the right situation for a happy, healthy, successful life of love and commitment. This method is practiced throughout the majority of the AMBC approved breeders, and I couldn't be happier about it. Very rarely are the wrong pups placed with the wrong families, thus helping prevent homeless, sheltered, or abused AMs. I only wish the rest of the animal breeding programs in the world took this same approach. It really does prevent the "Christmas puppy" syndrome where families add furkids to their gang, only to drop them off at the pound when they realize what they got themselves into. This especially happens when a new movie comes out that features a particular breed (think of Dalmations, Labs or Great Danes), and then everyone wants the dog from the movie. With a breed the size of an American Mastiff, this is extremely important! Adding a human-sized dog to your family is a huge responsibility, pun intended, and every step taken to ensure you are ready for one is of the utmost priority, including open farm days, contacting local owners, researching hte AMBC, joining the American Mastiff Family Forum and even reading this book!

After going through this process a second time to add Ludo to my family, I couldn't be happier. Ludo was equally easy to house train, socialize, and obedience train. His personality matched up perfectly with what I wanted in a dog. He is confident, bold, loyal, super friendly, and loves everything in life. I should also mention, Ludo is as bull headed as they come, but balances it out with a greater amount of love and eagerness to please, which is all you can ask for out of Man's Best Friend. To this day, Ludo is about 20 months old, is a healthy 195 pounds and growing, sharp as a tack, and the biggest love bug anyone could ever meet. He goes wherever I go and meets new people all the time who melt in his paw.

About a year ago, we went to an AM party at our friends', the Bradfords, house in South Carolina. It was an amazing day filled with fur, food, and loads of fun. At this party, I was able to hang out with the Nowak family who are the proud guardians of Vayda, Ludo's full sister and littermate. Missy, Vayda's mom, planted a bug in my ear about doing a book with all the images I shot of American Mastiffs. The thought had crossed my mind in the past, but I never gave it a second thought until the push

I received from Missy and friends. From that brainchild stemmed the goal of creating the first ever American Mastiff book, both informative and loaded with images, much like a coffee table book. The objective was to make a true resource readily available to the public about this great breed while being able to show off the many American Mastiffs across the country through photography. Groundwork was laid, schedules were created, emails were sent, and before I knew it, Ludo and I were on the road.

Our journey took us through the entire east half of the United States and even up into Canada, eh. Along the way we met some great people, made some life long friends, played with beautiful dogs, and took in some of the great scenery this continent has to offer. Ludo and I were like Maverick and Goose, Starsky and Hutch, or even Bill and Ted as we embarked through our excellent adventure. Meeting over 50 American Mastiffs and their families was quite the task, but one I wouldn't trade for the world. Being able to share stories, trade information, learn about new toys, and hear all the amazing stories was a true once in a lifetime opportunity. My only regret is not being able to cover the west side of the United States. This was at a time when I was going through my divorce and relocating to the Midwest which decreased the amount of time I originally allocated for the whirlwind trip. It is my goal to visit all those families and breeders that I missed, at some point in Ludo's life.

At the moment, Ludo and I continue to grow together; him in size and me as a person. We continue to adventure our way through this world as a team. He has recently adopted a little brother from the shelter, Carlos, the Cairn Terrier. To see the two of them play is to see the true nature instilled in both breeds. Carlos is a true terrier when he is in play mode with Ludo, and Ludo takes certain measures to ensure he doesn't crush Carlos. If you asked either one of them who was the bigger dog, they would look at you in confusion and shrug their shoulders. They get along better than human siblings, and rarely talk back. Ludo does like to sass me on occasion, and it's the funniest thing. With

the exception of play time, the pair of them are absolute babies, and love to lay around on their humans, or at least be touching them somehow. Ludo, my feet, Carlos, my lap.

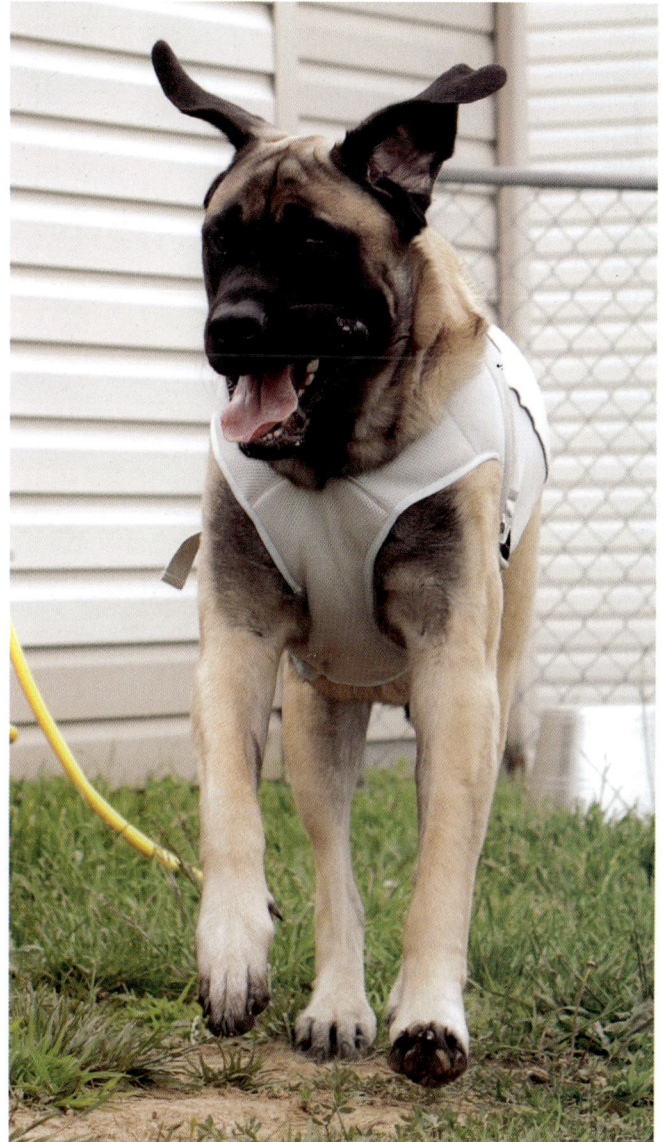

20 months

Left to right: Bueller, Jazz, Molly
Humans: Barbara, John

Left: Gus and Ludo roughhousing
Right: Gus giving us the Mastiff raspberry

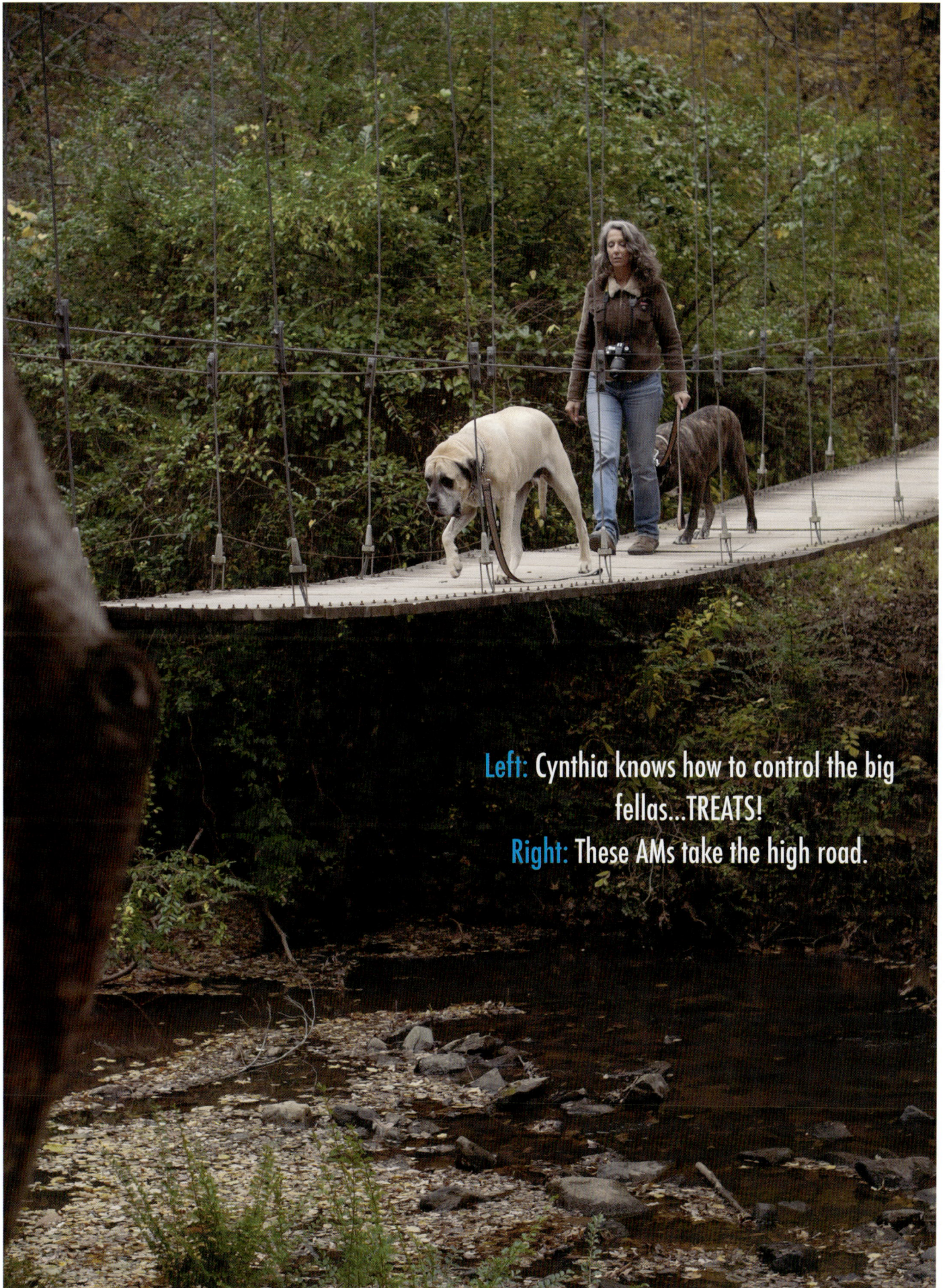

Left: Cynthia knows how to control the big fellas...TREATS!
Right: These AMs take the high road.

Left: (top) Gus, Brutus, Ludo (bottom) Gertrude
Right: AM train: Bueller, Jazz, Vayda, Ludo

Mastiff FACES!

These are some of the many faces an AM makes throughout the day. They display so many emotions and they can be quite comical. (above) Ludo, (right) Vayda

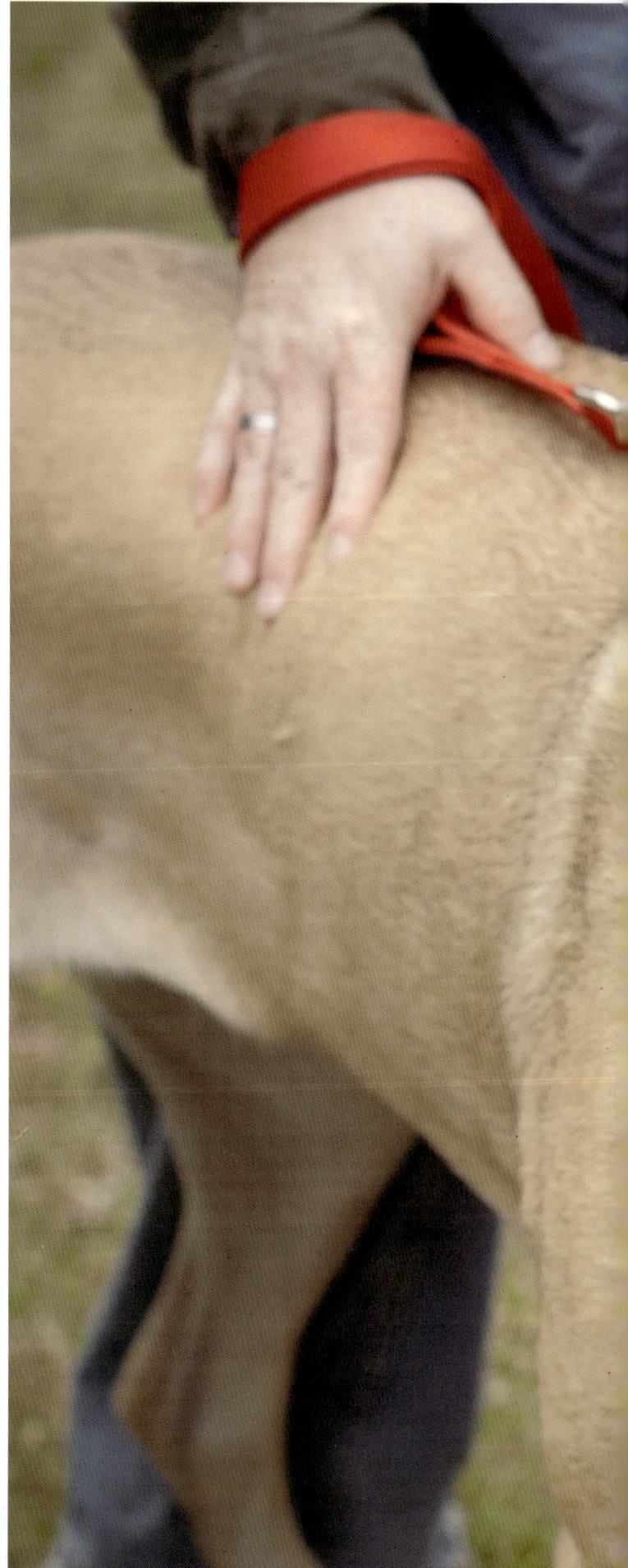

Left: Tiberius
Right: Kingston

Vayda: Still in her dorky teenager growth stage, Vayda shows us just how tall AMs can be. She clearly has no problem drinking out of the human-size water fountain. No puddle-sipping for this girl.

The water fountain's height is three feet.

Above:
Kyra with Bentley, the six-week-old Maltese.

Right:
Ludo and his buddy, Brody, hanging out on his Kuranda dog bed... typical little boys!

Left:
Cardhu,
the snow-loving
American Mastiff
in Canada.

Right:
Cardhu, R.I.P.
She was the Julien family's first AM muse. 2001-2010.

Now they have two more wonderful AMs, Roka and Islay.

Left:
Brutus and his sisters. As you can tell, Brutus is a total snuggler when it comes to his people.

Left: Ludo Above: Winnie and her playdates. Below: Lemon, the contemporary girl

BRINDLES

These are all great examples of brindle American Mastiffs.

Left: (top to bottom)
Kaiya, Kaiya (www.redleash.com),
Hudson
Above: Zoya
Right: Rocco doing his best Elvis
impersonation

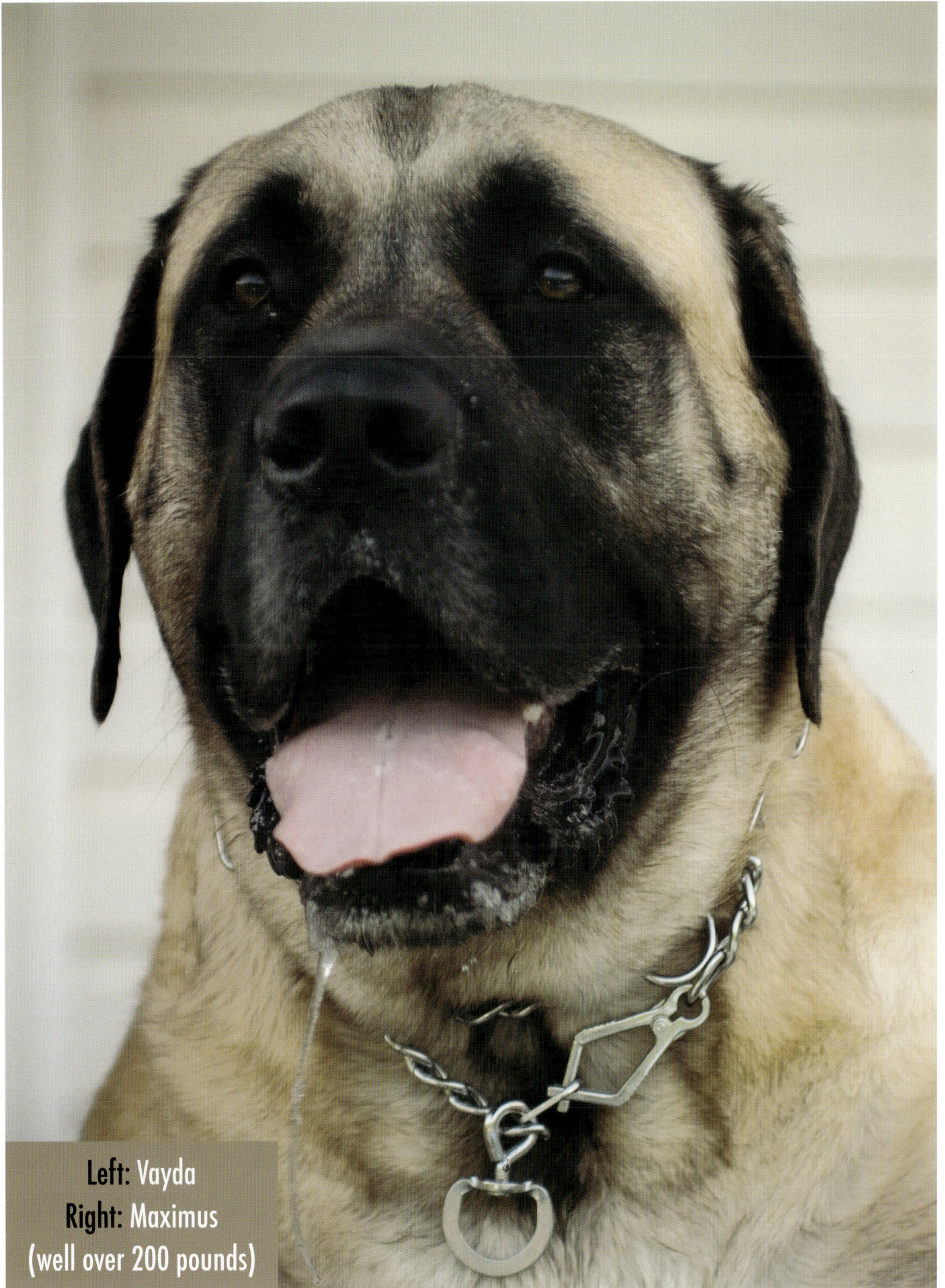

Left: Vayda
Right: Maximus
(well over 200 pounds)

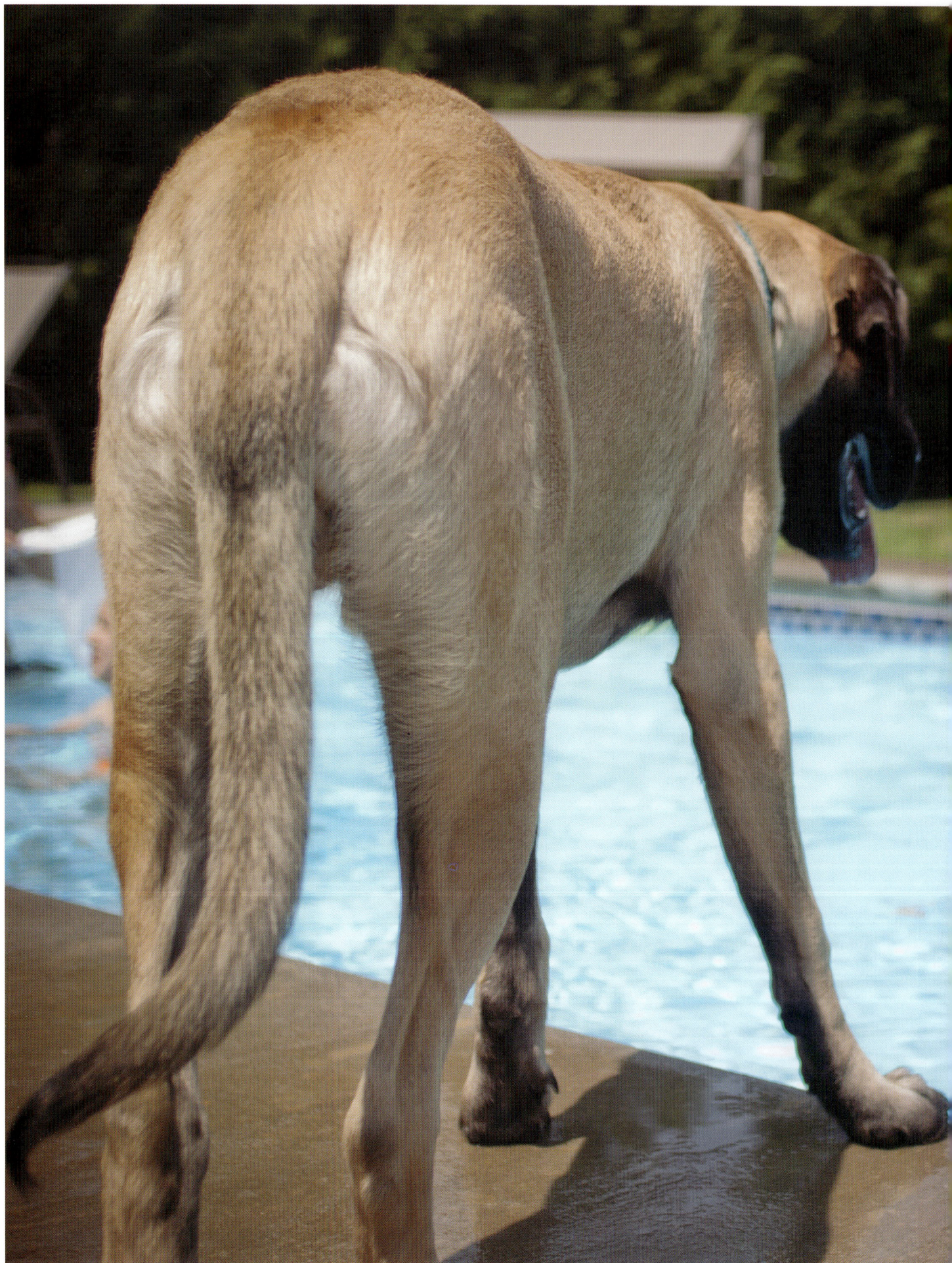

Mastiff Pool Party!
Left: Ludo on life guard duty
Right: (top to bottom)
Angus the waterfall dog, Maximus,
Angus and the crew getting splashed

Top Left: Murphy, Kingston, Ti
Right: Murphy, Ti, Kingston
Far Right: Ti meeting a horse
Bottom Left: Murphy
Bottom Right: Kingston and
Ti, the best brothers ever!

Murphy:

Murphy is from Ti's first litter. Tiberius belongs to Rachel Lamory, but has been kept intact per the request of Sycamore Creek for stud use. He occasionally makes the trip to OH from PA to handle his business. Murphy is a shining example of the quality pups he produces. At six months of age, Murphy is already around 100 lbs of solid muscle. Despite his enormous size, Murphy still knows his place in the pack and takes commands from even the smallest of his human brothers.

Open Farm Day

Orion Farms, to whom I owe thanks for my current AM Ludo, scheduled one of their open farm days in accordance with my book trip. The turnout was remarkable as AM families and potential future owners came from all over the north eastern area to be a part of a magical day. It was great for everyone to see siblings from their furkids' litters as well as talk about common goals, training techniques, funny moments, and a plethora of other topics that tend to pop up when we talk about our boys and girls. It's like being a part of an elite organization where only insiders understand the conversations. These moments almost always end in laughter, which is what our American Mastiffs are known for...making us smile.

With over 50 people in attendance, the event was spectacular and the Ware family were great hosts. Kevin Ware even gave a speech at one point that had all humans and furkids listening intently and enjoying the moment as over two tons of dogs were able to socialize, almost like a class reunion or wine social.

On the next dozen or so pages are images from that day, along with Orion's breeding stock. More information and images can be accessed online at www.orionamericanmastiff.com.

Thanks again, Ware family and friends, for Ludo, the party, and all the support you continue to give the American Mastiff community and me.

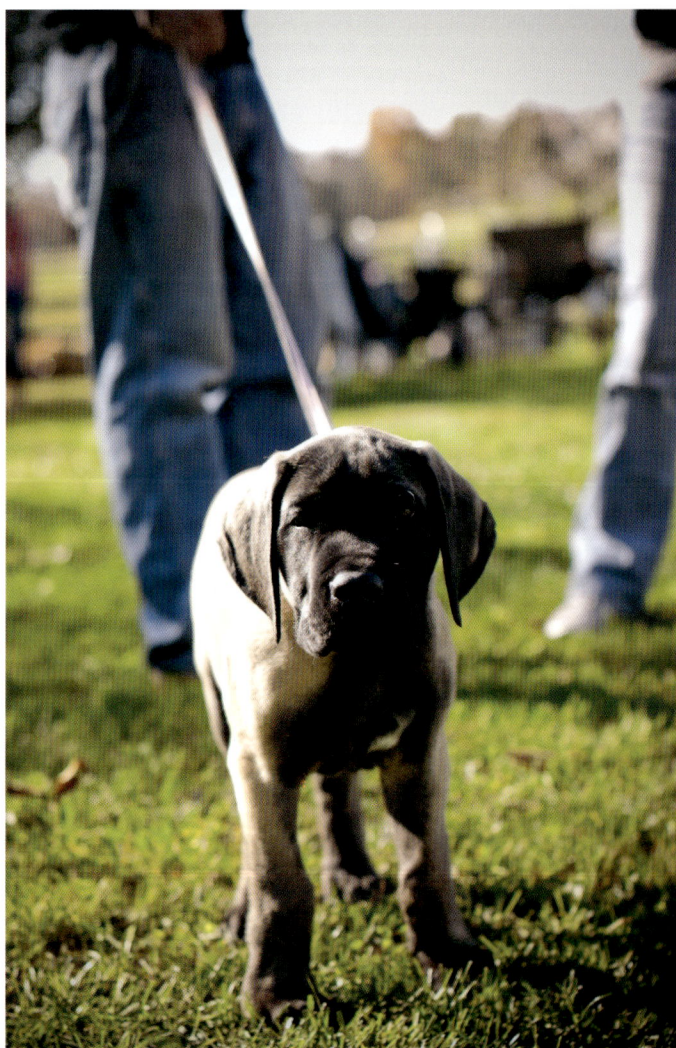

Above: Gabby
Right: Merlin (Ludo's dad) notice the similarities to Ludo. Merlin pups are usually pretty easy to spot.

ORION FA

AMERICAN

MASTIFFS

Above: Lily
Below: The AMs' signature amber eyes
Right: Bacchus

Mac and Bloo, brothers: Bloo (left) is a great example of a fluffy apricot

149

Left: Achilles
Right: Aprilia and Achilles

Left: Charli
Right: Dexter

Left: Nico (Deepwood)
Right: Achilles

Left: Cyno Right: Ludo hanging out with Lily and the Milo family

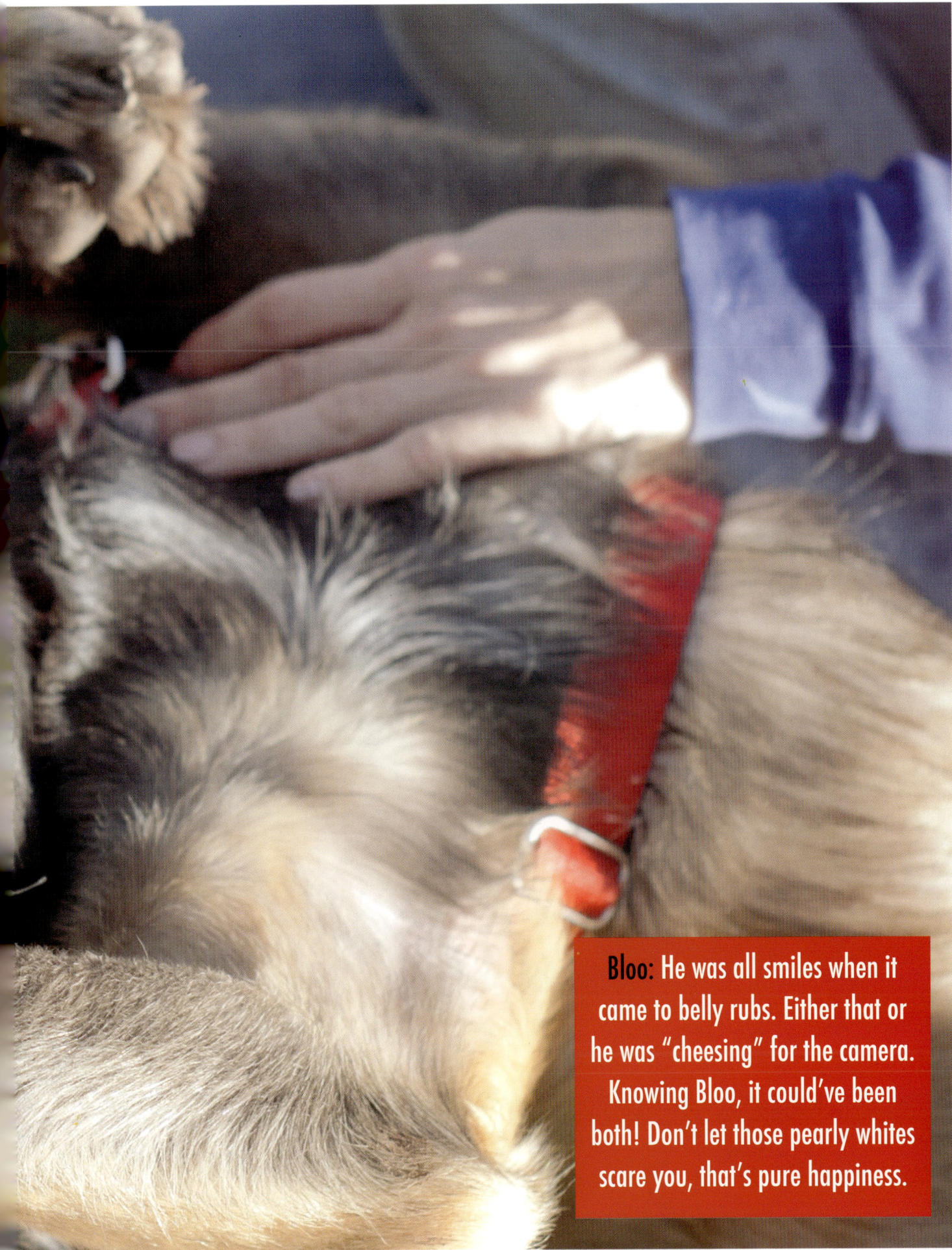

Bloo: He was all smiles when it came to belly rubs. Either that or he was "cheesing" for the camera. Knowing Bloo, it could've been both! Don't let those pearly whites scare you, that's pure happiness.

Moomba and her offspring (left to right): Bloo, Gaia, Moomba, Axle, Samson

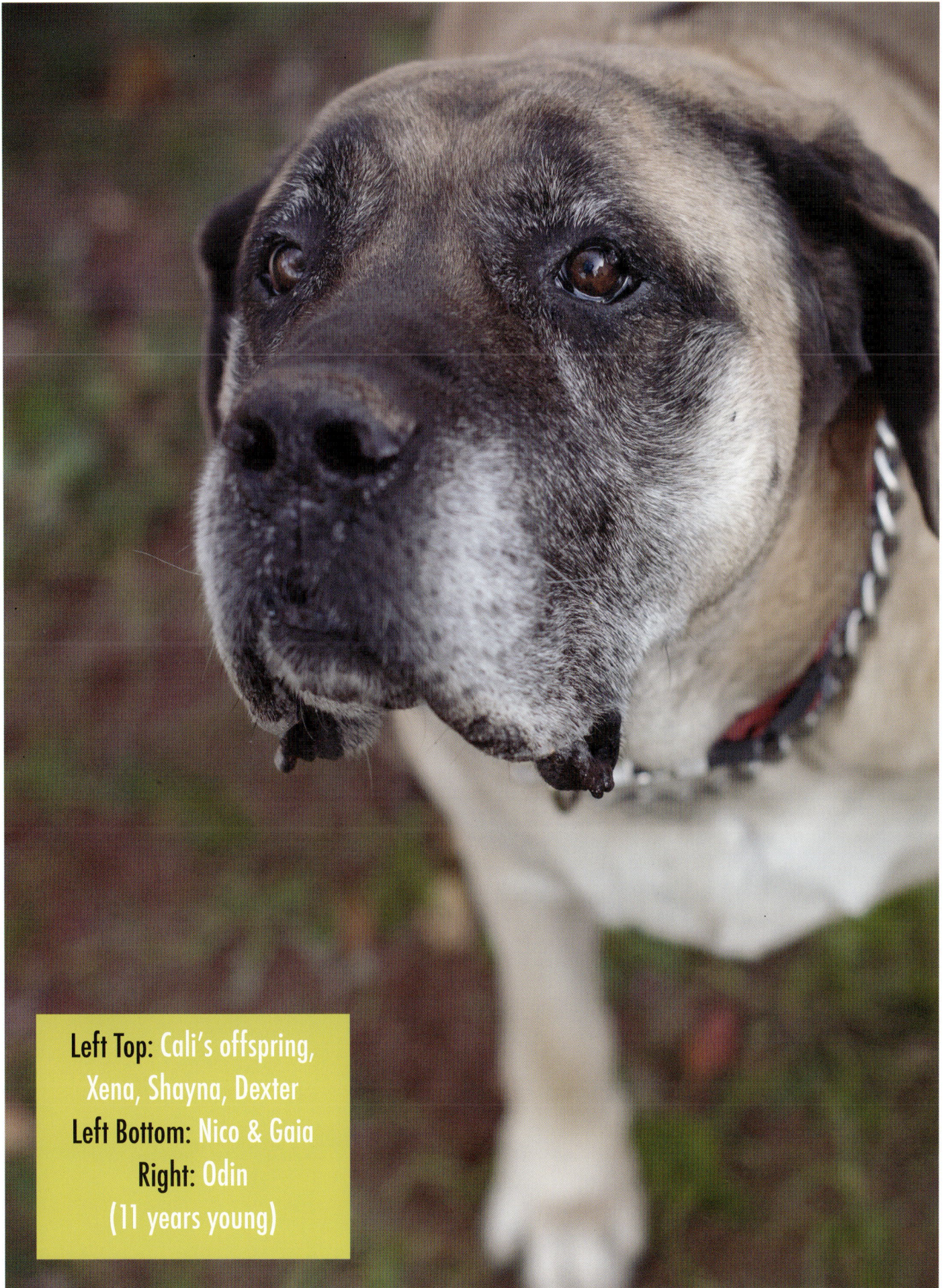

Left Top: Cali's offspring,
Xena, Shayna, Dexter
Left Bottom: Nico & Gaia
Right: Odin
(11 years young)

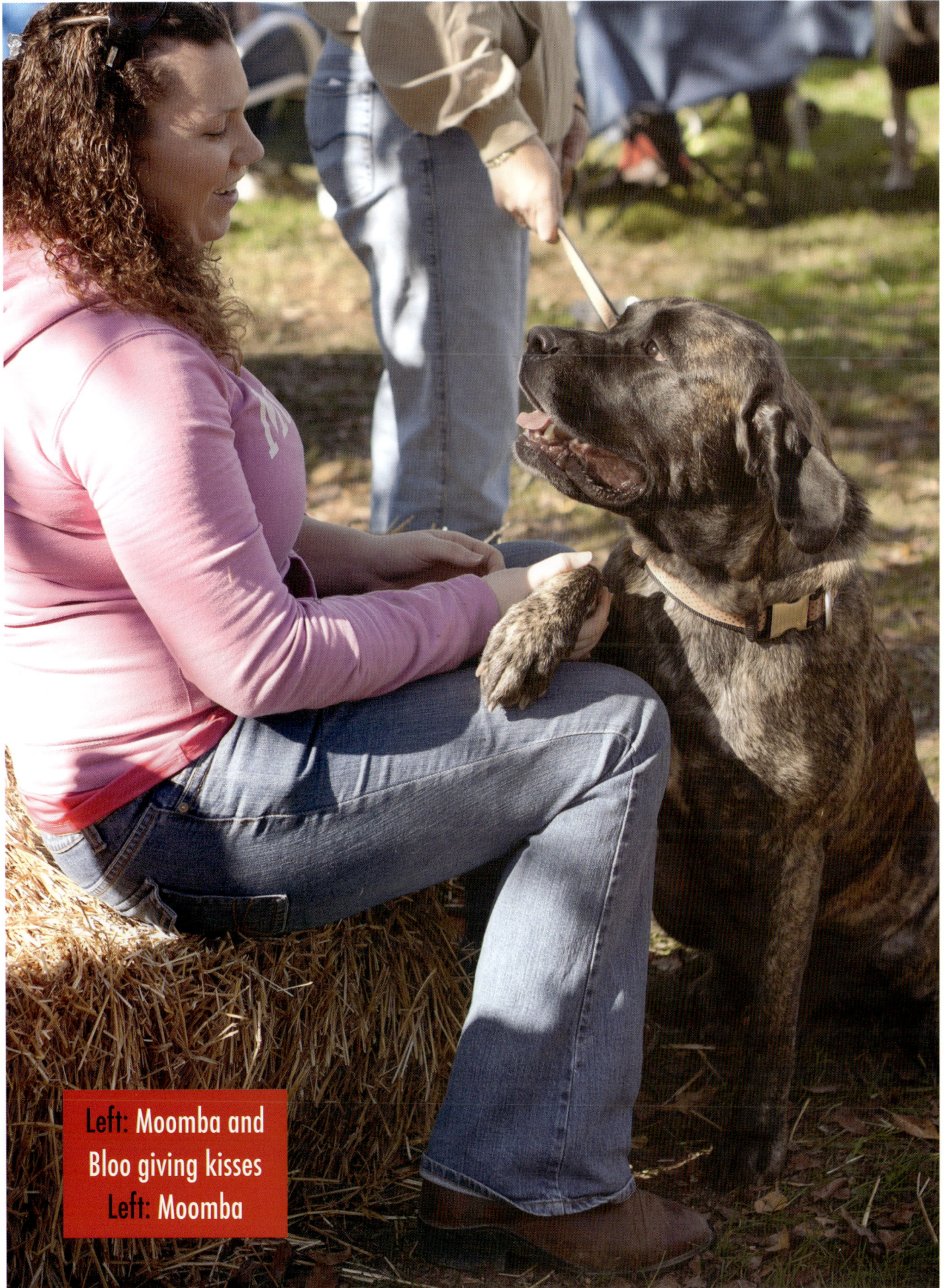

Left: Moomba and
Bloo giving kisses
Left: Moomba

Pandora's offspring (left to right): Atlas, Ludo, Duval, Cyno

Above: Gaia (the fluffy) **Right:** Lily
Below: Bloo
Far Right: Gaia, a future breeding dog of Orion Farms, and already primed for therapy work. She is so sweet and gentle.

American Mastiffs make
GREAT
Therapy dogs!

{ Many AMs across the country are TDI certified and visit hospitals, homes, U.S. veterans, libraries, and schools. }

ORION

AMER

MAST

Pandora

Minerva

FARMS

ICAN

IFFS

Merlin

Grendal

Cali

Left: Ludo **Top:** Vayda and Nathan. A therapy dog in her own right, her brother has been labeled as neurologically delayed & mildly autistic; Vayda is perfect around him. **Below:** Max

Vayda (left) Ludo (right): Brother and sister met in SC at the Bradford's house.

Both are from Merlin x Pandora (Orion Farms)

SWIMMERS?

While some AMs do enjoy the pool, others will look at you like you are crazy and transform themselves into a two-ton boulder (as demonstrated by Max, above).

If you do wish to get your AM into the water for recreation, I recommend starting off small with streams and creeks, then moving up to large bodies of water. Ludo hated the water when I took him in the pool with me, but he LOVES creeks and some lakes now (where there are ducks in sight). Kiddie pools are another way to introduce them to water. They tend to wade in it, drink out of it, and play with toys in it.

Right: Angus, on the other hand, LOVES the water, especially if someone is splashing him in the face.

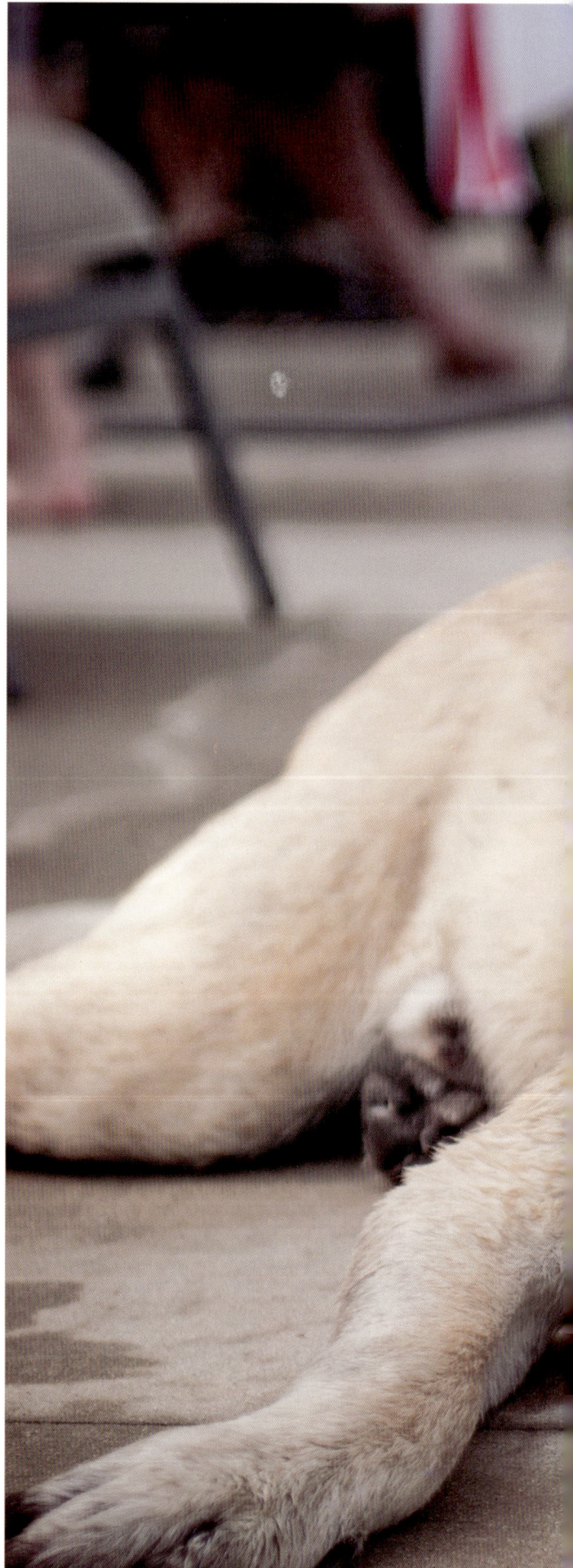

I'm All
EARS!

Below: Apollo at five months
Right: Fresca doing her model walk

{ AM puppies are notorious for their big, floppy, velvety-soft ears. They do eventually grow into them and make for some pretty amusing puppy moments. }

While AMs can appear fearsome to strangers, the humans "they own" see nothing but smiles! When AMs aren't running around like goofballs, they love to snuggle and give you "the look" as demonstrated by some of these love pups.

Above: Thunder demonstrates the "Pet me please" face.

Right: Archie demonstrates the "Holy cow I'm so excited to see you" face.

Opposite Page: Ludo showing the "What are you doing?" face.

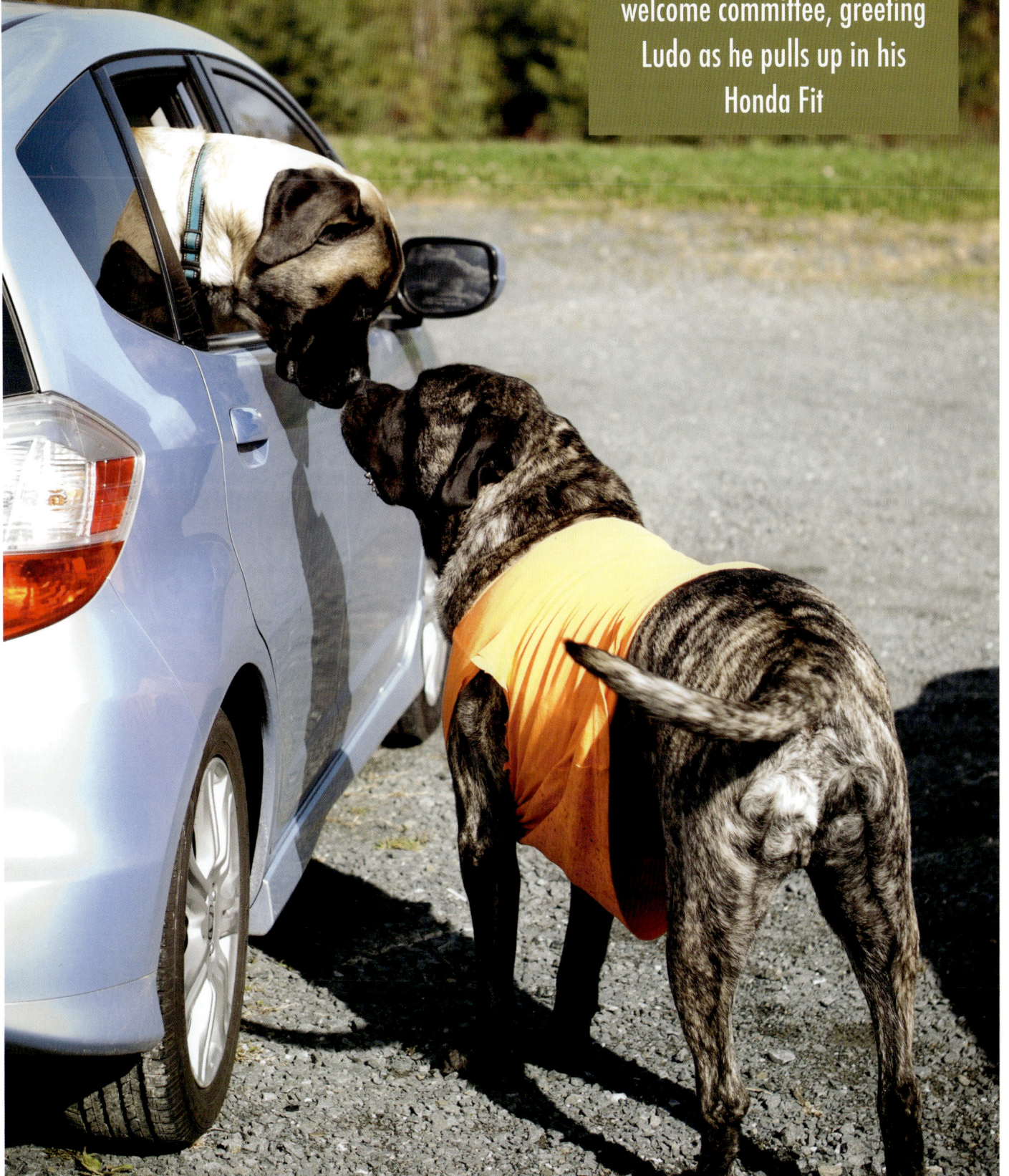

Left: Gryphon and Ludo enjoying the sand
Right: Archie, head of the welcome committee, greeting Ludo as he pulls up in his Honda Fit

Gryphon:

As a Navy dog, Gryphon loves the beach and catching some waves.

Starting at an early age, try to expose your AM to a vast array of textures, such as sand, water, rocks, grass, dirt, etc. The more textures and things AMs encounter and accept as puppies, the more "bulletproof" they will be in new environments as they grow older. No matter how bold and confident a puppy may seem, there will always be something he or she will encounter that causes uncertainty. It could be skateboards, statues, motorcycles, or even trashcans! When your AM is encountering something new, never let your pup get away with acting fearfully. Once you recognize what's causing your pup to feel intimidated, stick around long enough to check it out thoroughly. To do this well, you must be calm, confident and patient. There is a fine line between coddling and forcing, and success is where these two meet. Leaning to either extreme will often produce negative results. So keep your cool so that your pup can, too!

FiveBRanch
Terrell, Texas

Five B Ranch is the newest AMBC approved breeding family. Lisa Berberich and her family are doing a fantastic job representing the breed and community! This is just a small glimpse of their wonderful program.

These two crazy kids are Mac (left) and Bloo (right). Mac is a shining example of a fawn male with the standard short hair. Bloo, on the other hand, exemplifies both the apricot coloring and the "fluffy" gene. Some would say this makes Bloo very special, but ask Mac and he'll tell you, "he's okay for a little brother, I guess."

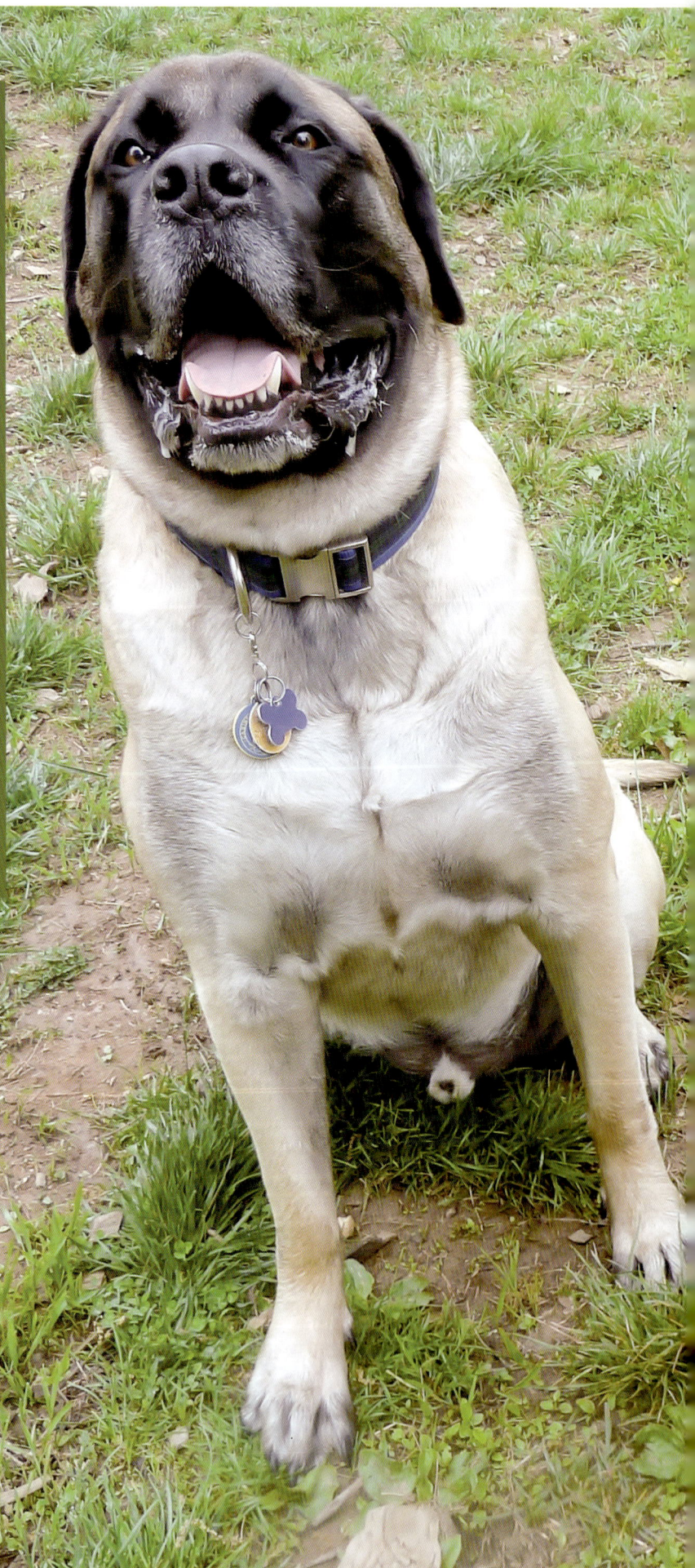

CRUISER
The Giant

{ By now, you know the "standards" of the breed and how males can be 200+ pounds on the high end. Well, Cruiser (above) is one of the examples of a GIANT. He may not seem any different than some of the other AMs in this book, but Cruiser weighs in at a whopping 245 lbs. He may not be the biggest AM out there, but he's one of the "biggies" indeed! }

Chief

{SycamoreCreekRanch}
Londonderry, Ohio

Mato

Marjan

Tocho

Personal Story from: Desirée C. Kerr

"Winnifred"
What's in a name...

When I tell people my dog's name, I am often met with looks of confusion, amusement or even disdain. I have a knack for choosing ridiculously long, obscure, eye-roll-inducing names for my dogs (as Grizelda and Antigone would confirm, if they were still around), but Winnifred seems to be the most perplexing to people, especially to our new neighbours in Basel, Switzerland. It appears that the German language has no use for the 'w' sound we cherish in English, so my dog's name is instantly transformed into something barely recognizable that sounds like Veeneefrayed. Add the fact that the only similar name with which Baslers seem to be even remotely familiar is Winfried (a masculine name), and we end up with a pseudo-bilingual-Germglish argument about the gender of my dog (never mind her age, which they never believe), almost every time we're out an about, which is usually two or three times per day. You would think my German would be perfect by now!

So, why did I bring all this trouble on myself? First of all, when I met my little pup for the first time back in October, 2010, I had no idea we'd be making the move to Switzerland. I wanted to pick a very American name, in honor of her heritage, and I almost went with Martha (Washington, Stewart, et al.), which means 'lady', but it just didn't suit her. Other finalists were Lucille (as in Ball and like B.B. King's guitar), which means light, and Lola (which, unfortunately, is short for Delores and means 'sorrows'), but they just seemed too feminine and delicate for the brave, inquisitive, intense little ball of pudge who adopted me that day. Winnifred was not even on my list but by the time we got home, she just reminded me so much of Winnie the Pooh (both in looks and personality), and I thought of Winnifred Harper Cooley, the American author of The New Womanhood way back in 1904 (she was a bit of a trailblazer who fought for women's rights before the phrase even existed), and I was sold. I think the name technically means 'friend of peace', but I've also heard 'joy and peace', which is nice and hopefully attainable someday, since Winn is anything but peaceful at this stage. Winnifred does approach life in a very Pooh-like manner, taking things that come her way in stride and making the most fun possible out of everything she encounters, and she's also a bit of a tough cookie and a trailblazer, in her own right, like her namesake Miss Harper Cooley.

Regardless of my original reasoning, Lady Winnifred seems to have embraced her name and I wouldn't (or couldn't) change it now for all the world. A truly spirited young lady, Winnifred is not yet peaceful but she feels, exudes and creates more than her fair share of joy every single day. Thank you, bold and beautiful Winnifred, for sharing your life with me and for answering to your unique and perplexing mouthful of a name (at least most of the time)!

Winnifred is the first and only American Mastiff in Switzerland. Recently moving from Canada, she has made quite an impression on her new community!

197

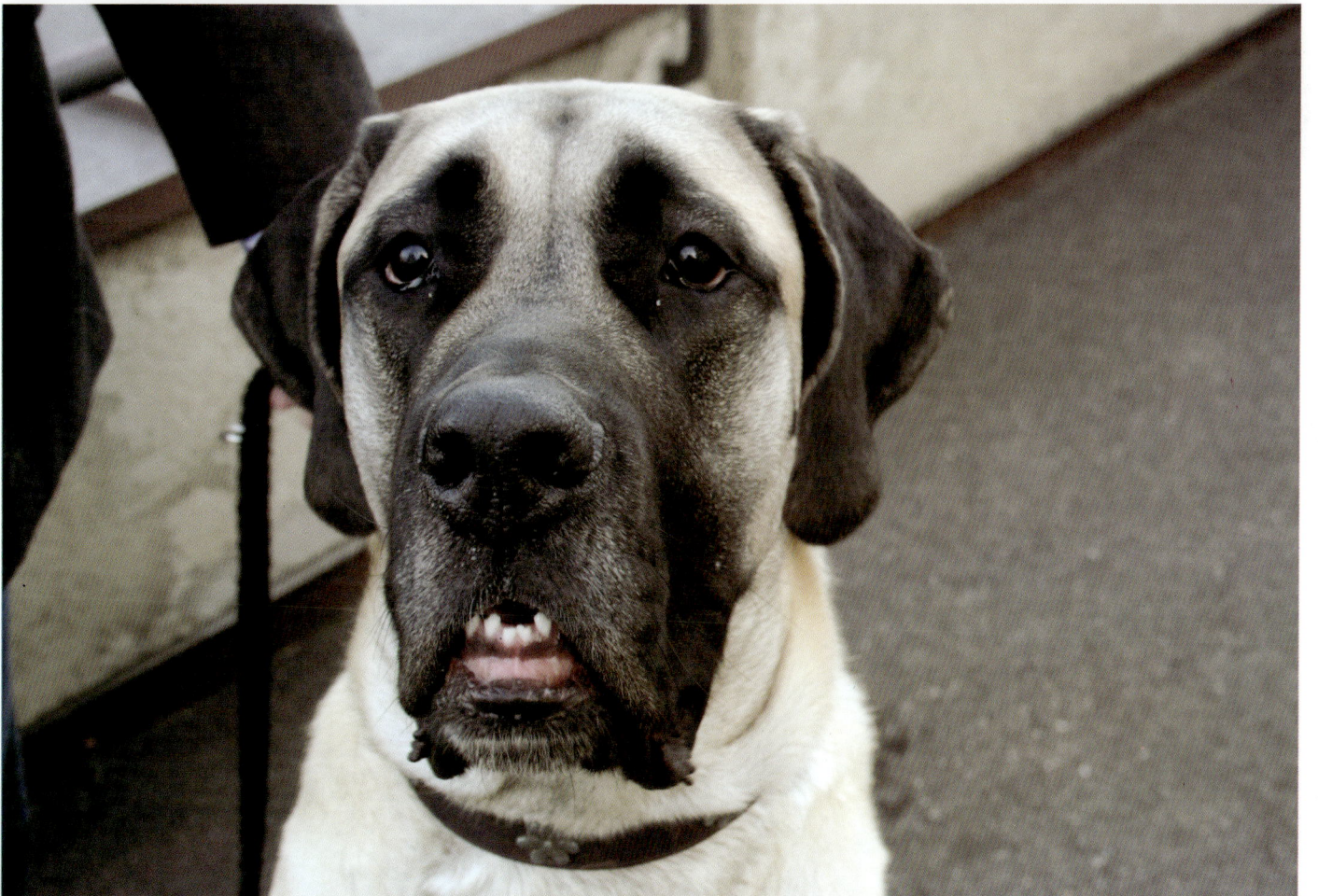

Personal Story from: Beth Bull

"Georgiana Beatrice Bull"

"Beatrice" means 'bringer of gladness,' and she sure has been that from the moment we met her! Georgiana comes from three of my favorite British novels (Jane Eyre, Great Expectations, and Pride and Prejudice) in honor of the AM's British heritage. My husband wanted to name her Montana, where he spent summers on his grandfather's organic wheat farm growing up, so we are hoping to have a male AM in the future who will get that name. Georgie was born at Orion Farms to Calliope and Merlin on February 10, 2011.

Georgie is a sweet, affectionate and playful puppy! She is not an alpha dog at all, but Kathy told us when we picked her up from Orion that she was the first puppy in her litter to figure out how to get out of the puppy pen...and she has continued to perform Houdini-like tricks

chewing her nylabone, when the bone rolled away from her and she did not want to get up to go get it...so she made that noise she makes that means "Mommy, help me!" At the very same time, my husband Rob, who was on the other side of the room was asking me to come help him with something. I went to Georgie first, as it only took a second to give her the bone...but then my husband started teasing me, saying: "Oh, I guess a person has to make that noise to get attention in this house!" - and he began imitating Georgie's cry for help noise. Well, Georgie heard that, and before I knew it she was painfully raising herself to her feet and walking over to the other side of the room to check on Rob. Rob felt terrible when he realized what she was doing! But that puppy (at 10 months old) was making sure he was alright.

We could not love our Georgie-girl more! And we are hoping to add another AM to our family in the not-too-distant future. Thank you for taking the time and effort to put together

ever since. And she LOVES people! One of my favorite stories about her loving nature is from the day after her spay and stomach tacking surgery when we first brought her back home. The poor baby had 32 staples in her tummy and was on pain meds. She would lie down very carefully and then, understandably, not want to move. She was laying on our bedroom floor

the first book on these wonderful dogs! We couldn't imagine our lives without our Georgie! And we will display the book proudly for all those who, meeting Georgie, become interested in the breed.

Georgiana shows that big dogs can run fast too...and sleep even faster!

"Hurley"

We had to make the agonizing decision to re-home our Chihuahuas because our autistic son could not handle the high pitch of their barking. However, our hearts and home felt empty without a dog. We did a lot of research among breeds and breeders, and exposed our son to various sizes and types of dogs to see which, if any, he would be able to tolerate. We discovered that the deeper barking had no effect on him. Once we found that out, we then went on to research larger breeds. When we stumbled across the AM, we felt like we had solved our problem. At first glance, we thought that they were gorgeous, but reading the stories of how great they were with kids, even (and perhaps particularly) special needs children, and about their amazing temperaments, sold us on the breed. From the moment we brought Hurley home, he fit into our family as though he was meant to be a part of it. He's phenomenal with our two small children, and steals the hearts of all he meets. Even as a small puppy, he instinctively knew how to be gentle with our kids. We've seen our son come out of his shell in a way we hadn't thought possible since we added Hurley to our family. We knew that he would tolerate the dog, but for him to love him as much as we do truly speaks volumes about what type of dogs the AMs truly are. In addition to being the easiest puppy we've ever had to train, he is very intelligent and every bit as loving as he is big. We're astonished by his growth, because each day he's larger than the day before, and so is his personality. He's becoming somewhat of a local celebrity, because if you know an AM, you are in love with an AM. He is truly a joy and we are forever thankful that we found our wonderful breeder and the absolute perfect breed (and dog!) for our family.

"Sahara Lucy"

Sahara Lucy is 21 months old as I write this. The only story I can think of is that we just adopted her about four months ago from Flying W Farms. We flew from Dallas up to Ohio, rented an SUV, went and met her and drove with her all the way back to Dallas! She has been the MOST perfect, sweetest, gentlest dog we could have hoped for! We were planning on getting a puppy from Five B Ranch in Terrell, but were joking about how cool it would be if we could bypass the hard puppy stages.then I decided to wing it and post a request on the AM Facebook group to see if anyone knew of any possible AMs up for adoption, even though I knew it was almost unheard of...and someone posted something about Sahara and directed me to the forum to check out more info. WE JUST LOVE HER, she is the most well behaved girl (and she's still "technically" a puppy!) - walks RIGHT by your side on a leash, doesn't tear anything up in the house, never takes anything from counters... we just can't say enough good things about our girl.

Hurley (right page) is a shining star for the breed's therapy capabilities.

Sahara Lucy (left page) is a great example of those few instances where an AM is looking for a new home. While very rare, sometimes our AMs need re-homed due to family structure changes or unsuitable home environments. In these cases, inspiring people like the Seymour family come to the rescue! It's a win-win for both humans and furkids alike.

Personal Story from: Scott Heaney

"The Lemon in my water"

I had wanted an American Mastiff for some time, after researching extensively and finally finding a breeder here in Canada, Popular Bluffs Ranch. The waiting list was around a year long, and I could hardly wait! Unfortunately, in the fall of 2008 I was struck with an illness that really altered my life. It wasn't life threatening, but it was bad enough that I was in chronic pain and, as a result, had developed severe depression. I deliberated whether I should go ahead with my plans to get an American Mastiff, as I wasn't sure I could give her the care she would deserve. After some serious thought, I decided to go through with it, and boy am I ever glad I did. But what was I going to call this beautiful girl? Sadie? Daisy? I didn't want to go with something so common. How about Lampshade? Suzanne? I just couldn't decide. In the Spring of 2009 while anxiously awaiting her arrival, I was sitting on my back deck going over this question in my head and looking at pictures the breeder had sent of my pup. During that time, the only thing I could really drink during recovery was water with lemon. As I sat there, looking at her picture, I reached for my water and it hit me. Lemon! Picking her up was one of the happiest days of my life. She made me forget about my pain and became the best therapy anyone could ever ask for. Lemon became an integral part of my recovery and even today she still helps distract me from the less severe pain that occasionally takes me by surprise. Having her to care for refocused my life.

203

Personal Story from: R.C. Albergo

"Bixby Consequence"

A fairly cool name for a fairly cool dog. But Bixby is so much more than that. She was brought into our "pack" to serve as a disability service dog, and we learned that she would also be an invaluable diabetic dog, although we had no idea at the time that American Mastiffs were intuitive of certain human conditions, like diabetes. Her roll in this little pack of ours was set when it became apparent that I was going to need help retaining my independence, which is so important to me. After my seventeenth back surgery I began having what we call "gravity issues". I began falling and trying to get back on my feet was rather difficult. That's where a service dog would come in handy. Being able to use the dog as a sort of perch to push off of, I could once again be on my feet.

We knew this dog would need to have an easy temperament, be social and strong... make that very strong. As research progressed an associate brought pictures of his gorgeous American Mastiff by to brag... I simply fell in love and knew this was the gentle giant for me! Our research brought us to Cameron Pridmore and the Capell Creek Kennels.

In the year plus that we've had Bixby, our focus has been basic command training and an exaggerated socialization submersion. She's accompanied me to the hospital several times, she loves grocery shopping and just walking through the local marina. Without formal training she has been able to recover me from several falls by simply blocking walkers from colliding with me, she'll "post up", and allow me to use her to once again find my footing.

One shocking thing about the AM, is their sixth sense. It was never discussed as a need, but she knows when my blood sugar drops and forces me to stop what I'm doing to remedy it. It started when she was only four months old. She found a piece of exposed skin (I was wearing shorts that day), licked the back of my leg and proceeded to bound off to play in the yard I was mowing. Over the course of an hour, she came by a few times to say hi. On her fifth pass she sat right in front of the mower, not moving as she had done earlier. I thought she just wanted to go get a drink in the cool house, and with the headache I had it sounded good to me! Upon reaching the house I noticed just how out of sorts I felt. After taking my blood sugar, I was shocked to find that it had dropped to a dangerous 36 mg/dL, so not good! A snack to raise my sugars and a "cookie" to reward the dog, I immediately sent a text message Cameron's way.

Much to our surprise, my husband and I learned what a brilliant decision we made in our selection! According to Cameron, more and more information is starting to surface as to how intuitive AM's truly are. As valuable as she is as a service dog, she is also so fiercely loyal to her "friends", her best friend is a thirteen pound Miniature Pinscher, named Ziva.

Ziva's human called scared and worried that her much loved "Zee" had gotten out of the house in the middle of a rain storm. It was decided that Bixby would lead the search. Walking around in the driving rain, telling Bixby to find Ziva. We would call out Ziva's name and Bix would, in the lowest end of the baritone scale would "woo-woo" for her buddy. Less then an hour later, a soaking wet, shivering Zee came out from under a car right behind her buddy Bixby, jumping up into mamma's waiting arms!

The Art of AM

Art and pets have been synonymous for centuries. Over the last three decades, the same has held true for the American Mastiff. As an artist myself, and alumni of the Art Institute of Atlanta, I am always in awe at the creativity put into the love of our pets. From paintings that capture a special moment in an AM's life to memorials created to give new life to a passed family member, artistic creativity remains a huge part of the American Mastiff community. Beyond traditional art, the AM family displays skill sets in collar fabrication, custom-sized costumes, beds, pillows, dishes, and, of course, photography. An American Mastiff coming into your life is like having a muse for all things artistic.

"HALEY"

Haley 2012

Above: Barbara Bradford's black and white painting of Bueller.

Left: Holly Clark-Dull's emotional driven watercolor of Haley, an AM that has gone to the "Rainbow Bridge".

Right: An unfinished portrait of my first AM, Lurch. This is a memorial piece for him titled, "You Rang?".

About the Auth

Born in Homestead, Florida, I was raised in a military family with a strong appreciation for animals and nature. Moving every two to three years, I learned to adapt in new environments, make new friends and to never grow attached to things that can seem, and often are, temporary. The constant in life for me was art, family and animals, particularly dogs. While I am a great friend and family member, I am an even better advocate to all animals.

After graduating from high school in Hampton, Virginia, I moved to Atlanta, Georgia, where I earned an Associates Degree in Graphic Design at the Art Instute of Atlanta. Soon after, I was Art Director for a women's magazine based in GA and enjoying my craft. After 9-11-2001, I began to weigh my options, not to mention my three-year mark was coming up. After three years in one place, I begin to itch until I find a new place to call home. My decision at that time became clear and I joined the Air Force in the Visual Information field. I was a Cameraman by trade, but also continued with my graphic design and even expanded my horizons with photography. The five years I served in the military proved to be the greatest adventure of my life. I traveled the world, worked in Europe, Africa, and the Middle East alongside all of our military branches, experiencing cultural diversity directly. I have to admit, there is nothing comparable to being in the Sahara Desert with a group of Marines. I learned pretty quickly what life was all about and how humanity is so vast and different, while at our core we are equals. You would never think a person could grow accustomed to the sound of alarms, gunshots and missle attacks, but to thousands of troops, a handful of nations, and millions of people, it's the normality of life and a standard of living. While I do not support war, I will never turn my back on my fellow troops continuing to serve, nor a person from any culture extending a hand in need.

After my time in the service I got married to another service member, moved to Hawaii, then again to Georgia where I adopted my first and second American Mastiffs, Lurch and Ludo. While being a newly appointed father to an AM, I was also taking advantage of my GI-Bill to further my education working towards a BA and Masters in Business. Over the next couple of years my marriage deteriorated and I divorced in late 2011. Lucky for me, I was used to moving. Ludo and I hit the road and headed to southern Indiana, staying with family while finishing up school. Immediately following the move, we began our road trip to create this book. I was at a point in my life where an adventure with my boy Ludo was exactly what I needed. The tour proved to be beneficial for both of us, as Ludo and I really experienced our journey as a migration toward a new life. A two-man wolfpack if you will, Zach Galifianakis.

Currently, I have my BA in business and am a year away from finishing my Masters Degree. Ludo has gained a recue terrier, Carlos, for a brother, and the relationships with my life-long friends as well as new ones are stronger than ever. From here forward, I want to experience life from a new perspective everytime I wake up. I no longer strive to be rich, base success on money, or try to position myself atop the ranks of peers. My goal now is to live simply, and as naturally as possible, with minimal effort devoted to a stressfull existance. Once my savings account runs dry from self-publishing this book and eating, the real journey begins...

I have always felt a stronger connection with animals and nature than with humanity itself. While people change, animals remain constant in their motives and livelihood. You can always rely on animals to act like themselves, while humans remain unpredictable. Traveling the world I've noticed only one constant: animals represent family, purpose and life.

Right: Kona enjoying the first snowfall of the year. Erik couldn't ask for a better model as he continues to expand his photography portfolio.

Below: Hudson is one enlightened pup.

Above: Islay in one of my favorite Rob Julien images. Below: Maddox

Below: Huxley & Samson on their memory foam bed. Another great option!

References

AMBC APPROVED BREEDERS

These breeders have voluntarily agreed to abide by the ethical breeding guidelines and rules of the AMBC. These are breeders of the true purebred American Mastiff dog which trace their bloodlines back to Flying W Farms, Inc.

Flying W Farms American Mastiffs
Fredericka Wagner
Founder of the AM breed
President of the AMBC
PO Box 845, Piketon
OH 45661
740-493-2401
Fax: 740-493-0072
www.flyingwfarms.com
flyingw@bright.net

Sycamore Creek American Mastiffs
Connie Hammond
Chairperson and
Vice President of AMBC
Londonderry, OH
740-887-2111
www.Sycamorecreekam.com
sycamorecreekranch@yahoo.com

Five B Ranch
Lisa Berberich
AMBC Secretary
Terrell, TX
972-551-1437
www.fivebranch.com
lisab@fivebranch.com

Hidden Acres Farm
Diane St. Martin
13 Pleasant St., Southampton
MA 01073
413-203-1319
www.hiddenacresmastiffs.com
hiddenacresfarm@charter.net

AMBer Pines Farm, LLC
Sandy Berger
6610 Reside Rd, Imlay City
MI 48444
810-614-8956
www.american-mastiff.com
sandy@american-mastiff.com

Capell Creek Ranch & Kennels
Cameran G. Pridmore
1490 Capell Valley Rd
Napa, CA 94558
707-257-2957
Alt: 707-363-7998
www.capellcreekKennels.com
lotsaminis@aol.com

Deepwood Acres American Mastiffs
Jim & Sandy Taylor
North East, MD 21901
410-398-0769 evening/weekends
www.DeepwoodMastiffs.com
DeepwoodMastiffs@hotmail.com

Fantastic AMs
Louis Meng, Jessica Wang & Andrew Meng
Shanghai, China
louismeng@gmail.com

Orion Farms
Melanie and Kevin Ware
Reymar, MD
410-756-1507
www.orionmastiff.com
Orionmastiff@hughes.net

Poplar Bluff Ranch
Bob & Wynona Young
P.O. Box 384
White City, Saskatchewan
Canada S4L 5B1
306-771-4516
www.americanmastiffcanada.com
b.wyoung@sasktel.net

Ramega Farms Giant Breeds Kennels
Rafael Garcia III
Barangay Palo Alto
Calamba, Laguna
Philippines
Website: http://giantbreeds.mypets.ws/giantbreeds_wp/
giantbreeds@yahoo.com

*Breeders insist on puppies going only to loving homes where they will be part of the family. They are easily housetrained using the same training methods used for any puppy. They want to live in the house and be part of the family. They are content and happy when with their family.

The American Mastiff Family Forum:

This is your one stop shop for all questions before, during and after you have an AM as a part of your family. It is like the library of congress for American Mastiffs and Families.

http://amfamilyforum.net/ Forum/

Board Owner:
Michelle Parlier
Username: MParlier
Email address:
MichelleParlier@yahoo.com

Full Moon Dog Training
Justine Oakwood
Founder / Trainer
www.fullmoondogs.com
fullmoondogs@gmail.com

LIVE, LIFE, LARGE
fashion accessories for your AM and other furkids!
Kathy Dutterer - Founder
www.livelifelargecollars.com

FACEBOOK PAGES:
"American Mastiff Family" group page.

"The American Mastiff"
This is the book product page. Updates of new products, charity events, and recourses can be found here.

*Some AMBC breeders also have individual pages dedicated to their programs. Searching their company name is the best way to find them.

Contributing Photographers:
Albergo, Rosemary (204)
Allen, Eric (128 Brutus)
Ardizzone, Amber (44)
Baker, Kathy (181)
Berberich, Lisa (189, 190)
Billig, Heather (11 Ellie)
Bradford, Barbara (206 Bueller, 207)
Bransky, Adrienne (46 Huxley&Samson, 210 Huxley&Samson)
Bull, Beth (199-200)
Clark-Dull, Holly (205)
Coradini, Michael (133 Zoya)
Diomataris, Ashlee (46 Hurley, 202)
Dutterer, Kathy (79)
Frailer, Lori (183 Thunder)
Gerber, Joanne (67)
Giesing, Ed (194)
Gross, Lori (Red Leash Pet Photography / www.redleash.com) (133 Kaiya X 2)
Heaney, Scott (203 Top image)
Helm, Trevor (58, 77)
Hobbs, Jamie (209)
Hulme, Whitney (203 Bottom two images)
Irene Salek-Raham (40 Ruthie)
Julien, Rob (41, 42, 43, 128 Cardhu, 195, 196, 210 Islay)
Kennedy, Thomas (127 Kyra)
Kerr, Desirée (27 Winnifred, 85 Winnifred)
Lopez, Marty Lizama (11 Aprilia & OP, 191, 192)
Lopez, Walter (193)
Marton, David (198 Winnifred)
Mitchell, Anne (45, 210 Maddux)
Seymour, Jen (201)
Sonanini, Evelyne (130 Winnie and group, 197 Winnifred)

Swarts, Maria (14)
Walker, Katie (19 Optimus Prime, 46 Optimus Prime)
Warren, Angel (52 Keevah)
Weil, Stephanie (11 Morgan)
Zartiga, Joel (27 Titan)
Zotter, Erik (59, 210 Kona)

Contributing Writers:
Albergo, R.C. (204)
Bull, Beth (199)
Diomataris, Ashley (201)
Heaney, Scott (203)
Kerr, Desirée (197)
Seymour, Jen (201)

Credits:
Flying W Farms (5-6)
The AM Family Forum (29-33)

American Mastiff Breeders Council (AMBC)
"To protect, preserve and promote the true purebred American Mastiff"

AMERICAN MASTIFF WORLD PRESS

AMERICANMASTIFFWORLD.COM